SEA WAR IN THE PACIFIC

Marshall Cavendish

Published by
Marshall Cavendish Books Limited
58 Old Compton Street
London W1V 5PA

© Marshall Cavendish Limited 1978 – 84

ISBN 0 86307 166 X
Printed and bound in Italy by New Interlitho SpA.
THIS VOLUME IS NOT TO BE SOLD IN AUSTRALIA OR NEW ZEALAND.

CONTENTS

SEA WAR IN THE PACIFIC

Ignited by the attack on Pearl, war blazed through the Pacific in a cruel and brutal battle for freedom

From the end of the nineteenth century, Japan made no secret of the fact that she was bent on spreading her influence beyond the islands of her homeland. She intended to take by diplomacy, infiltration, or by force, lands in Asia and island groups in the Pacific. In 1940, the US began to exert strong political and commercial action to combat Japan's aggressive activities, so much so that she sent diplomats to try to come to terms with the West.

The US Government knew of impending aggression against the Dutch East Indies and the British colony of Malaya through the decoding of Japan's secret military and diplomatic messages and reports of invasion convoys at sea. Moscow was informed by its agent Richard Sorge that he thought Japan would attack Pearl Harbor, but was not sure of the date.

Our first feature tells the ever-incredulous story of that grim day at Pearl Harbor on 7 December 1941. The attack, thrust home with great accomplishment and effect by Vice Admiral Chuichi Nagumo, was the overture to a conflict in the Pacific of enormous extent, unutterably brutal in its disregard for human life, incredibly wasteful in aircraft, shipping and munitions losses and expenditure, and conducted on a scale undreamed of by the most inventive of military fiction writers.

The aggressor shows foresight

A large part of the success of the Japanese aggressors as they swept through the islands of the Pacific was due to the Imperial Japanese Navy, and especially to the great carrier fleet (in 1941 the world's largest) which the Japanese had had the foresight to build up, beginning with the *Hosho*, a mere 7,470 tons, launched in 1921, and ending with the gigantic 62,000-ton *Shinano*. But without two aircraft, the Nakajima B5N 'Kate 'and Aichi D3A1 'Val' the carrier fleet would not have been the hard-hitting force it was. Our second article shows the development of this twin strike force.

Paradoxically Japan also built the world's greatest battleships, *Yamato* and *Musashi*, each 64,000 tons of 'unsinkable' naval might. The third feature in this book tells their inglorious story. It illustrates the enigmatic thinking of Japan's strategists: on the one hand they had developed a highly successful carrier fleet, with first-class protection from destroyers, submarines and cruisers, while on the other they conceived naval warfare in traditional terms, with huge battleships thundering immense broadsides at their enemies.

Typical of the war at sea in the Pacific was the Battle of Santa Cruz, between 70 US and Japanese ships and 400 air-

The 13,380-ton Japanese cruiser Nachi *sinks in Manila Bay after being hit by planes of Task Force 38 on 5 Nov. 1944. (Inset) Grumman Hellcats on USS carrier* Intrepid.

craft in late 1942. It is our fourth feature. The carrier USS *Hornet,* responsible for launching the Doolittle Raid against Tokyo, was lost, with a destroyer; many Japanese units were damaged. The damage could be repaired, but for Japan the disaster was the loss of experienced aircrews in 100 planes.

By late 1942 the Japanese momentum had run out. Seaborne lines of communication were being stretched to breaking point. Burma, the Philippines, Wake, Guam, Malaya, the Dutch East Indies, New Guinea, the Solomons — all this territory needed holding, policing, and supplying. As the successes of the US carrier forces and warships mounted, the Japanese defensive ability dwindled. By mid-1943, as Burton Graham, in 'Tarawa', our fifth feature, points out: 'The tide had turned'. This coral atoll in the Gilberts, with Betio the larest island, strongly fortified and manned by over 4,800 veteran Japanese soldiers, was a miniature fortress. It took four days, 3,000 US casualties and the annihilation of the Japanese garrison.

MacArthur's determination

One of the great themes of the Pacific war was General Douglas MacArthur's grim determination to return in triumph to the Philippines. He had stemmed the Japanese advance in New Guinea and begun to advance along its north coast. In May 1944 Biak stood next on the island-hopping policy which had proved successful in the drive towards the eventual goal — Japan herself. Biak, much larger than Betio, was thought to be lightly defended. But its garrison of over 11,000 included 4,000 seasoned combat troops, a tank company and naval infantry. Defensive artillery included 4.7in naval guns and a 6in gun, with many weapons up to 90mm. The landing was unopposed but the island's capture told from p. 46, took nearly four weeks.

While the reconquest of the Philippines was taking place, the Central Pacific drive initiated at Tarawa was switching north and nearing Japan. At the northern tip of the Marianas sits the black sanded volcanic island of Iwo Jima. It is a name which carries all that is evocative of the bitter and bloody island assaults in World War II. Our last article describes the assault, begun on 19 February 1945, and taking four weeks of some of the most gruelling close-combat fighting ever known. At the end, over 3,500 Marines lay dead in the black ash, together with 20,000 Japanese.

On 6 August 1945, a B29 Superfortress, called 'Enola Gay', piloted by Colonel Paul Tibbets, took off from Tinian, in the Marianas. In its bomb bay was the 9,000lb 'Little Boy'. When the first A-bomb exploded at 2,000ft over Hiroshima it heralded a new dimension in warfare. It also avoided massive casulaties in brutal assaults on the Japanese mainland. The next A-bomb destroyed Nagasaki. Japan gave in. The war was over.

Ford Island, Pearl Harbor, as it appeared to the attacking Japanese pilots just before 0800 on 7 December 1941. In the right-hand background can be seen the Pacific Fleet's oil supplies, which miraculously escaped destruction.

PEARL HARBOR

Japan's brilliantly successful attack on the US Fleet. And war came to the Pacific in horror beyond belief

'All hands, general quarters! Air raid! This is no drill!' The alarm sounded for an attack that was to kill 2,403 American citizens as well as cripple her Pacific Fleet. But the Japanese attack on Pearl Harbor on 7 December 1941 was the key that released the unrivalled military might of the US. The eventual fate of the fascist powers—both east and west—was sealed.

Japan's strike at Pearl Harbor is often presented as a surprise attack on the US Navy, yet relations between the two countries were so strained because of Japan's colonizing policies it was practically inevitable that, for Japan to get her expansionist way in Asia, she would have to use force against the US.

In May 1940 the US Pacific Fleet was moved from San Diego to Pearl Harbor. The Fleet had been taking part in maneuvers off Hawaii the previous month and was ordered to stay in Pearl Harbor by Roosevelt when the exercises were finished. This decision did much to spur Japan into signing the Tripartite Pact with Italy and Germany the following September.

By mid-1940 it seemed that the fascist powers were everywhere triumphant. Nazi Germany controlled the better part of Europe and looked menacingly towards Britain from the coast of France. Meanwhile, Imperial Japan was locked in her expansionist war with China—a conflict of almost unsurpassed brutality. America was deeply involved in the fight against the aggressors in both theatres and short of military intervention was giving all possible help.

Public opinion in the US was deeply split over whether or not to go to war, with the majority firmly in the isolationist camp. But President Franklin D. Roosevelt saw clearly enough that unless the dictatorships were defeated the US's own independence would eventually be threatened.

On 27 September 1940 Japan joined the Axis when she entered into a tripartite pact with Germany and Italy. Under the terms of this agreement 'the leadership of Japan in the establishment of a New Order in Greater East Asia' was acknowledged. By this time Britain had been pressured into closing an important life-line to China—the Burma Road. America imposed a partial embargo on exports to Japan. This embargo was later intensified and anything regarded as a strategic war material was included in the restrictions.

It soon became painfully clear in Tokyo that Japan's empire-building conquests in Asia could not possibly continue for much longer without the raw materials of war—especially oil.

Stunned US Navy personnel try vainly to clear up the mess of a shattered airfield on Ford Island after the Japanese first wave. The Pennsylvania-*class battleship USS* Arizona *blows up in the background, after breaking in two.*

Relations between America and Japan continued to deteriorate into 1941 and an armed clash appeared increasingly likely. But US naval strategists did not think an attack on Pearl Harbor at all likely. According to them, such an action would be an impressive but rather pointless piece of sabre rattling—yielding Japan no great benefits. It was for the same reason that the Japanese rejected the idea when it was proposed by Admiral Isoruku Yamamoto in September 1941. Its lack of any military value apart, an attack on Pearl Harbor would snap the already strained relations between the two countries and all-out war would result.

Yamamoto—himself opposed to war with America—kept his faith in the viability of his plan. He had put the finishing touches to this as early as the spring of 1941. But for the attack to succeed, Yamamoto realized that absolute security was essential. There was in existence a crypto-graphic code which enabled Japanese naval officers to communicate with no risk of American interception reading their messages. Another risk to security in a venture of such importance was the inevitable prolonged argument and counter-argument within the Japanese High Command. The chances of a 'leak' were enormous, so Yamamoto bypassed the High Command altogether and approached Emperor Hirohito's brother Prince Takamatsu, then a navy staff officer based in Tokyo. He was intrigued and told his brother, who gave the go-ahead for the idea to be studied in secret.

As relations between Japan and the US went from bad to worse, Yamamoto trained his men. The harbor at Kagoshima was chosen for dummy dive-bombing and torpedo dropping because the lie of the land was similar to that of Pearl Harbor.

In late July the French were pressured into handing over Southern Indochina to the Japanese. America retaliated promptly. Japanese assets in the US were immediately frozen and the partial embargo already imposed on strategic material was made total. Britain and Holland joined in the economic boycott. The stark choice facing Japan was certain economic collapse or an armed clash. War with the US was no longer a question of 'if'—only 'when'. Unless the flow of oil was swiftly resumed Japan would have to abandon the Chinese mainland—an intolerable loss of face for the military. The absolute deadline for a solution was October.

Talks were held throughout the summer and autumn of 1941. Cordell Hull, American Secretary of State, made his country's position clear—all sanctions would be lifted only if Japan took her forces out of China and Indochina. But the negotiations were nothing but a device for buying time. Hull knew perfectly well that Japan would never accede to such a demand. Despite the pleadings of the Japanese Prime Minister, Prince Fumimaro Konoye, the Emperor and War Minister General Hideki Tojo refused to countenance any compromise. They were convinced of Japanese invincibility against all comers. 'The day after war begins we will have to issue an Imperial Declaration of War. Please see to it' Emperor Hirohito told his Lord Privy Seal, Koichi Kido, on 13 October.

Also in October, the US was warned of a planned strike on Pearl Harbor by an unusual source. Richard Sorge, Moscow's master spy in Tokyo, had passed the information to Josef V. Stalin, who in turn had informed Washington. But American naval strategists still considered an attack on Pearl Harbor unlikely.

Anxious for a peaceful settlement with the US, but outnumbered in the cabinet and overruled by his emperor, Prince Konoye resigned as Prime Minister on 16 October 1941. The extreme hawk Gen. Tojo took his place. At this point the Japanese Ambassador in Washington, Kichisaburu Nomura, asked Tokyo to recall him. His request was refused and the expert diplomat Saburo Kurusu was despatched to buy time by supervising yet another round of 'negotiations'.

At this point it is worth speculating whether President Roosevelt was really ignorant of Japan's aggressive intentions. Apart from Richard Sorge's warning, the President also had access to *Magic* information—the decoded transcriptions of Japanese secret messages. It has also been suggested that Churchill thought that a Japanese attack on Pearl Harbor would demolish the case of the isolationists and bring America into the war and that Roosevelt agreed.

On 5 November Japan decided to make one more diplomatic approach to Washington before unleashing the now fully rehearsed attack on Pearl Harbor. This approach was sure to fail and was not intended to succeed—merely to give Japan the international veneer of 'peacemaker'. Presuming the breakdown of the talks, the Japanese Supreme Command's operational orders ended with: 'War with the Netherlands, America, England inevitable; general operational preparations to be completed by early December'.

Also on 5 November, the US Chiefs of Staff (Army and Navy) met Roosevelt to discuss the Far East. A month before, Generalissimo Chiang Kai-Shek, the Chinese Nationalist leader, had pleaded with America and Britain for help. US Secretary of State Cordell Hull feared that any further aid to China would provoke Japanese retaliation and General George Crook and Admiral Harold R. Stark urged the President to tread carefully. But it was resolved that if Japan undertook any military action against British, Dutch or US territory, America would intervene militarily.

After this decision the November talks between the two sides had no meaning whatever. Japan demanded a totally unacceptable retreat from America's stated position and tied her diplomats to a deadline of 29 November. This came and went with nothing resolved.

The force destined to attack Pearl Harbor had left Japan almost a fortnight before the 29th and congregated at Tankan Bay in the Kurile Islands. It was a powerful force— six aircraft carriers and nine destroyers, with tankers and supply ships, two cruisers and two battleships in support. Twenty ocean-going submarines acted as an advanced guard. Five of these were equipped with two-man midget subs. This force, commanded by the brilliant Vice Admiral Chuichi Nagumo, was the cream of the Imperial Japanese Navy.

On 26 November, the strong armada left the Kuriles and set course for Pearl Harbor—adopting a route that would bring them towards the US Pacific Fleet from the north. Japanese 'met' forecasters had told the task force that the weather was expected to be bad in the regions it would pass through. This would make the necessary refuelling tricky, but if they approached from the north there was less chance of being spotted by the Americans.

By 6 December, American naval strategists were still saying an attack on Pearl Harbor was most unlikely. Their grounds for such confidence were the unequivocal reports from US and British reconnaissance planes that Japan was launching a full-scale amphibious operation in the south and Japanese ships laden with soldiers were reportedly entering the Gulf of Siam. American opinion could not accept the idea that Japan was capable of mounting two naval operations at the same time.

As dawn broke on 7 December, the Japanese carrier force had reached a position 275 miles north of Pearl Harbor. Fifty-one Aichi 'Val' dive-bombers, 43 Mitsubishi Zero-Sens 'Zeke' fighters, 40 Nakajima B5N2 'Kate' bombers with shallow-running torpedoes and 50 high-level 'Kates' left the decks at 0600. Eighty Vals, 54 Kates and 36 Zeros followed up.

USS TENNESSEE (1943)

USS Tennessee *escaped more lightly from the Japanese attack than some of the other US battleships. Along with* Maryland, *she was moored in 'Battleship Row'. Both were protected on the seaward side by* Oklahoma *and* West Virginia. *This meant that* Tennessee *escaped being torpedoed. But she did suffer two bomb hits. The first struck the center gun of turret 2, cracking the barrel and putting all three guns in the turret out of action. The second smashed through the roof of turret 3, damaging the structure and the rammer of the left gun.* Tennessee *was hastily repaired and was ready for service in just under a fortnight after the attack— 20 December 1941. At the*

The ships lying at anchor at Pearl Harbor were charged to keep a 'Condition 3' state of preparedness. Every fourth gun was supposed to be manned. But as America still regarded herself precariously at peace, none of the main guns was manned and the ammunition for the MGs was in locked boxes. The keys were in the charge of officers—some of whom were not even on duty.

A boatswain's mate saw between 20 and 25 aircraft approaching at 0730 but he could not see who they belonged to. All doubt was dispelled when the first bomb dropped just before 0800. Pearl Harbor's naval commander, Admiral Husband E. Kimmel, got the news of the attack three minutes later. Naval air commander, Rear-Admiral Bellinger, broadcast the words that were to smash the isolationist grip on America: 'Air Raid, Pearl Harbor, this is no drill!'

Even the ambitious Yamamoto could scarcely have hoped for a more total surprise attack. The US Pacific Fleet was caught with its pants well and truly down. Blunders and bad luck brought about this American debacle. One certain blunder was when two NCOs, manning a radar station, saw Japanese planes closing in and watched them for 40 minutes. They tried to raise the alarm by telephone, but failed to contact anybody who believed their report. USS *Ward* gave another warning at 0645 when she sank a midget submarine at the mouth of Pearl Harbor. This too was ignored.

'Tora-Tora-Tora!' ('Attack, attack, attack!') Commander Mitsuo Fuchida, in charge of the first wave, signalled to his airmen at 0749. Six minutes later the bombs began to fall. Their target was Battleship Row—eight battleships at the SE of Ford Island. Low-flying torpedo Kates roared in on the hapless ships. Four of them were holed or damaged in five minutes. While the Kates punished the vessels below the waterline, Vals were busy smashing decks, bridges and gun turrets. Other Kates were finishing off the job with high-level bombing.

The initial attack inflicted shattering losses on the Pacific Fleet. USS *Arizona* (32,600 tons) blew up and snapped in two. More than 1,000 men were drowned. The carnage continued when three torpedoes smashed into *Oklahoma* (29,000 tons). She turned over—imprisoning what was left of her crew below decks. When holes were later cut in her bottom only 32 survivors crawled out. A total of five hits—four torpedo, one bomb—put paid to the 31,800-ton *West Virginia*, while the *California* (32,600 tons) blazed for three days after fires reached her fuel tanks. Then she sank.

USS *Nevada* (29,000 tons) tried to steam out of the harbor, but Japanese bombers caught her and she finally beached on a mudflat at the entrance to the harbor. *Maryland* and *Tennessee* escaped relatively lightly. They were shielded from torpedoes by *Oklahoma* and *West Virginia*, which were moored on the seaward side. The 33,100-ton flagship of the US Pacific Fleet, *Pennsylvania*, was in drydock and was more of less unscathed at the end of the attack.

The old battleship *Utah* had been in use as a target ship for some time before the Japanese attack. Denuded of her superstructure, from the air she looked like an aircraft carrier. Japanese pilots expended valuable torpedoes on this worthless relic.

At the NW shore of the harbor Japanese aircraft damaged the light cruiser *Helena* and the seaplane tender *Curtiss*, while the light cruiser *Raleigh* was crippled. The minelayer *Oglala* was sunk. The destroyers *Shaw*, *Cassin* and *Downes*, the light cruiser *Honolulu* and the repair ship *Vestal* all suffered damage.

While the Pacific Fleet in the harbor was being pulverized,

---

end of the month she sailed for Puget Sound Navy Yard, Bremerton, Washington State, to receive more permanent repairs. The AA armament and the secondary battery were modernized at the same time. This work was finished by March 1942. The following September Tennessee *returned to Puget Sound to undergo modernization. Her superstructure was rebuilt and her machinery brought up to date. Modern flag spaces were installed as well as a combat information center. Modern radar and fire-control equipment was added. Armament was also improved with 5in/38, 40mm quads and 20mm singles being installed.*

After modernization, Tennessee *was active in the Pacific in World War II—seeing action off Tarawa, the Marshalls, New Ireland, the Marianas, Palau and Leyte Gulf.* **Laid down** *14 May 1917;* **Launched** *30 April 1919;* **Length** *624ft 6in.* **Beam** *97ft 3in (114ft from 1943);*

Displacement *33,000 tons (40,500 tons from 1954);* **Complement** *57 officers, 1,026 men in 1920 (90 officers, 2,219 men from 1943);* **Armament** *12x14in, 16x5in, 40x40mm, 43x20mm; Equipped with two aircraft in 1943 (one catapult);* **Speed** *21 knots.*

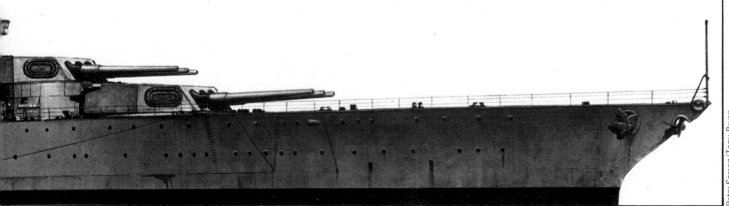

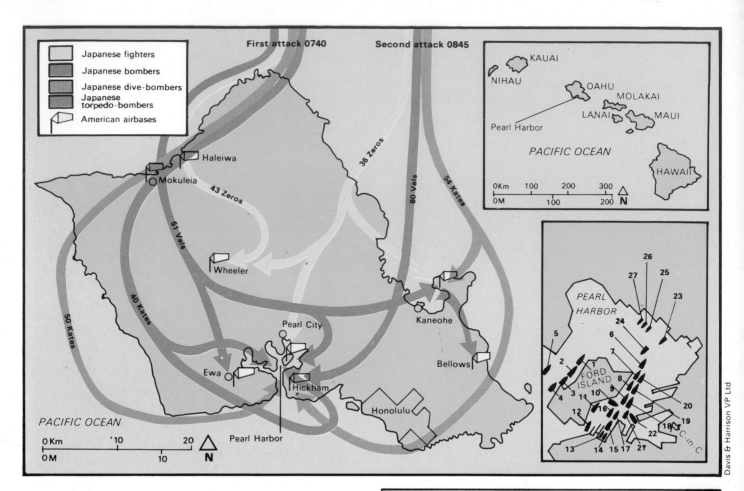

First attack 0740   Second attack 0845

Japanese fighters
Japanese bombers
Japanese dive-bombers
Japanese torpedo-bombers
American airbases

Haleiwa
Mokuleia
36 Zeros
43 Zeros
51 Vals
80 Vals
54 Kates
Wheeler
40 Kates
50 Kates
Kaneohe
Pearl City
Ewa
Bellows
Hickham
Honolulu
PACIFIC OCEAN
0 Km   10   20
0 M   10
N
Pearl Harbor

KAUAI
NIHAU
OAHU
MOLAKAI
LANAI   MAUI
Pearl Harbor
PACIFIC OCEAN
0 Km   100   200   300
0 M   100   200
N
HAWAII

PEARL HARBOR
FORD ISLAND
C-in-C

the airfields on the mainland were also taking a hammering. At the US Marine Corps' Ewa Field were 49 airworthy planes. By the time the Japanese were through with them only 16 remained intact. Kaneohe was a flying-boat base equipped with 36 Catalinas. After the attack an incredible 27 were complete write-offs while six others were severely damaged. This was one of the most punishing attacks on air bases in World War II. Of 148 first-line naval aircraft, at least 112 were destroyed, as were 52 out of the 129 Army planes. Thirty-eight American planes did take off. Ten of them were shot down.

The first Japanese wave then departed. Its attack had lasted 25 minutes. In that time thousands of American lives had been lost and millions of dollars worth of strategic weaponry destroyed. But there was more to come.

At 0845, 36 Zekes, 54 torpedo Kates and 80 high-level Kates provided Japan's second wave. But now the Americans had woken up and were a little more prepared. Shore batteries opened up as did still-serviceable ships' guns. Japan lost only nine planes in the first wave. In the second the score rose to 20 in return for little effect—its value being confined to finishing off already crippled installations. The submarine base escaped unscathed as did the fuel depot. Here was stockpiled almost as much oil as Japan had in her entire reserves.

President Roosevelt spoke of the 'day that shall live in infamy'. If it was, it was also a day of appalling military cost to the United States. The Japanese had lost 29 aircraft and 55 men. For this meagre expenditure 2,403 soldiers, sailors, airmen and civilians had been killed, 164 planes destroyed and six battleships and three destroyers sunk, while a number of others had been badly damaged. Apart from the dead, the Japanese left 1,178 wounded Americans in Pearl

◁ Main map shows the approach of the first and second waves of the Japanese attack. Inset (bottom), the US Pacific Fleet as it lay at anchor. *1* Detroit, *2* Raleigh, *3* Utah, *4* Tangier, *5* Curtis, *6* Nevada, *7* Arizona, *8* Tennessee, *9* Maryland, *10* Neosho, *11* California, *12* Shaw, *13* Cassin, *14* Downes, *15* Pennsylvania, *16* Helena, *17* Oglala, *18* Oklahoma, *19* West Virginia, *20* Vestal, *21* New Orleans, *22* San Francisco, *23* Pheonix, *24* Solace. *25, 26* and *27* were destroyers.

▷ The wrecked destroyers Cassin *and* Downes *in dry dock. In the background is the Pacific Fleet's flag ship USS* Pennsylvania.

◁ ▽*Navy C-in-C Pearl Harbor, Admiral Husband E. Kimmel (center).*

▽*A US Navy rescue launch rushes to a blazing USS* West Virginia *to take off the crew's survivors.*

▽ ▷*A Japanese midget submarine. USS* Ward *spotted one of these at the mouth of Pearl Harbor, but astonishingly her 0645 warning was ignored.*

Official U.S. Navy Photo

Official U.S. Navy Photo

Official U.S. Navy Photo

Harbor. The only section of the US Pacific Fleet to escape damage was its carrier force. It was not at Pearl Harbor at the time of the attack.

If the Japanese had sent in a third wave—as Cdr Fuchida wanted—there is little doubt that they could have totally devastated Pearl Harbor. But Fuchida did not have his way. Vice-Adm. Nagumo, the task force commander, believed that he and his men had done more than a good day's work and the effectiveness of the strike had certainly surpassed all expectation. His force turned tail and settled down to a quiet journey home to Japan.

At 1347 Washington time, news of the attack reached Cordell Hull. Abruptly breaking off the now pointless diplomatic wrangle he unceremoniously dismissed Nomura from his presence.

The isolationist grip on America was at last smashed and she was now at war with Japan. The attack on Pearl Harbor, while brilliantly successful in itself, unleashed the might of the US military machine against Japan, as well as her German and Italian partners. For Japan the end would not come until she was utterly demoralized and Hiroshima and Nagasaki had been flattened by the atom-bomb. The entry of America into the war ensured the eventual defeat of fascism in both theaters. **Paul Hutchinson**

'VAL' AND 'KATE'

This successful twin-attack carrier team cut its teeth at Pearl Harbor. But lack of aircrews spelled the end

At 1120 on 8 May 1942 15 torpedo-bombers and 33 dive-bombers broke through the fighter patrols and the screens of cruisers and destroyers around the American aircraft carriers *Yorktown* and *Lexington*. The attack-aircraft from the Japanese carrier *Shokaku* managed to score only one hit on *Yorktown*, with a 554lb bomb. But the six torpedo-bombers and 15 dive-bombers from *Zuikaku* reached a higher degree of co-ordination in their attack on *Lexington*. Two groups of three torpedo-bombers attacked, one from either bow—approaching in loose formation at over 250mph. At a thousand yards from their target the first three dive-bombers released their loads—one 554lb SAP and two 132lb GP bombs apiece, from 2,500ft up, in 50° dives.

Lexington's AA batteries—5in guns, 1.1in quadruple and 20mm single automatic cannon—concentrated on the torpedo-bombers, which released their weapons at less than 800 yards range. The first bombs bracketed *Lexington* with near-misses. Other dive-bombers closed in on the carrier at short intervals—harassed by occasional and inaccurate AA fire from the screen. Just two of the bombs hit, both 132-pounders—inflicting minor damage—but shock and vibration due to the many near-misses caused extensive superficial damage. Although *Lexington* tried to 'comb' the tracks of the torpedoes, the port and starboard attack gave her little chance of dodging the 45-knot 'fish' and she took one hit each side. One bomber was shot down after releasing its torpedo.

This first fully co-ordinated attack on a carrier by dive-

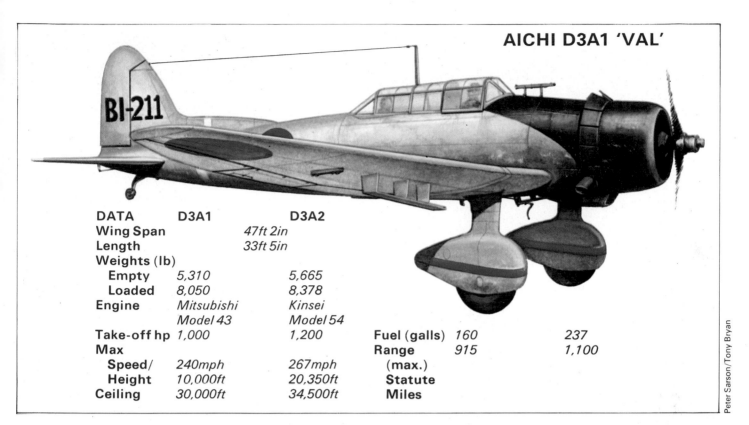

AICHI D3A1 'VAL'

DATA	D3A1	D3A2			
Wing Span		47ft 2in			
Length		33ft 5in			
Weights (lb)					
Empty	5,310	5,665			
Loaded	8,050	8,378			
Engine	Mitsubishi Model 43	Kinsei Model 54			
Take-off hp	1,000	1,200	Fuel (galls)	160	237
Max			Range (max.)	915	1,100
Speed/	240mph	267mph	Statute		
Height	10,000ft	20,350ft	Miles		
Ceiling	30,000ft	34,500ft			

Peter Sarson/Tony Bryan

Airview

The highly modified second prototype Aichi 11-Shi. A new power-plant, an 840hp Mitsubishi Kinsei 3, had supplanted the Hikari, but the production version had an improved Mitsubishi Kinsei 43, giving 1,000hp.

and torpedo-bombers had been carried out by the Type 99 Carrier Bomber and the Type 97 Carrier Attack Bomber, better known as the Aichi D3A1 (Val) and the Nakajima B5N2 (Kate). The code-names were given to the aircraft by the Allies, who felt the Japanese names would not 'stick' for identification purposes. By the time of the Battle of the Coral Sea in May 1942, these two aircraft types were responsible for the loss to the Allies of the British carrier *Hermes*, four battleships, two heavy cruisers, and more than 50 small warships and merchant ships. All this for the loss of only 72 aircraft in combat.

Credit for the development of the dive-bomber as a fighting weapon must go to the United States Navy. Small shipboard aircraft could not carry large numbers of bombs big enough to seriously damage warships if they were to be released in a level attack from medium altitude—relying upon a pattern of bombs from a number of aircraft in

formation. Trials during the late 1920s showed that by delivering a single heavy bomb at the lowest possible height —aimed by pointing the aircraft at the target in a steep dive —inaccuracies caused by errors of estimation of the target's speed and the wind speed and direction were minimized. So were the effects of evasive action on the part of the enemy. In 1929, the Boeing F4B-1 fighter-bomber went into service. It carried a single 500lb bomb for delivery in a steep dive attack. It was followed in 1930 by the first in the line of Curtiss 'Helldivers'—the 02C-1 two-seat dive-bomber/reconnaissance aircraft.

The Imperial Japanese Navy issued its first dive-bomber specification in 1931, but it was not until 1934 that the first 'Carrier Bomber' was actually ordered—Type 94 Aichi D1A1. The same basic design also served as the Type 96 Carrier Bomber, with the short designation D1A2—first dive-bomber (D), built by Aichi (A), second production

'Val's partner in the twin attack, 'Kate' Nakajima B5N2. This aircraft was different from the B5N1 by virtue of an improved power unit, the Nakajima Sakae 11, giving 1,000hp. Japan produced 1,149 Kates.

variant. Capable of carrying a 700lb bomb-load, this rugged biplane gained notoriety in December 1937, when it sank the American gunboat *Panay* and three merchant ships on the Yangtse River near Nanking.

Even as the D1A2 was entering production, the Japanese navy was issuing a new specification for its replacement. Aichi again tendered a design. This time a two-seat monoplane with a fixed undercarriage. The aircraft flew for the first time in January 1938. After the initial problems had been solved it was ordered in 1939 as the Type 99 Carrier Bomber, or D3A1. It was known to the Allies from 1942 by its code-name, 'Val'. Said to be derived from a German design, the D3A's debt to the Heinkel He 70 was small, the only noticeable similarity was the planform of the outer wing surfaces. With a loaded weight of under 3.5 tons, including over 800lb bomb-load and 1,300lb of fuel, 'Val' had a respectable performance. It had a top speed of 240-mph and was able to climb to 10,000ft in six minutes (faster than the Royal Navy's Fairey Fulmar fighter). The full bomb-load could be carried to a radius of 250 miles and beyond, with ample reserves for form-up after take-off and the attack and then the expected delay before the dive-bomber's turn to land on the carrier.

Flying trapeze

The big bomb—a 538lb or 554lb monster—was carried on an ejector arm. This was a sort of trapeze which extended to hold the bomb clear of the fuselage and the propeller arc. The two smaller 132lb bombs were carried under the outboard mainplanes. The bombs and two Type 97 7.7mm MGs installed above the engine and synchronized to fire through the propeller were all aimed by means of the pilot's telescopic Dive-Bombing Sight Model 2—a computing sight which calculated the angle of dive to make allowance for the path of the bomb after release. The movable rear gun was a Type 92 7.7mm weapon.

'Val' had excellent maneuverability once it had rid itself of the bombs. Many an Allied fighter pilot was unpleasantly surprised by its ability to look after itself in a dogfight. But there was no armor for the crew. They sat over 160 gallons of completely unprotected fuel. One hit even from a light-calibre bullet usually resulted in the destruction of the aircraft and the loss of the crew.

Up to 1934, all Japanese torpedo-bombers were of British design—although built by Mitsubishi. The first totally Japanese-made torpedo-bomber, the Type 92 Carrier Attack Bomber, was not successful. In 1937 this was replaced by the Type 96 (D4Y), designed by the Nakajima

company and built by the Yokosuka Naval Air Technical Arsenal. The Type 96 was officially regarded as an interim type, pending the development and acceptance of a monoplane design called for by a 1935 specification. But the reliable biplane was still in action over China until 1940. The monoplane designs, one by Nakajima and the other by Mitsubishi, appeared in 1937 and were both accepted for production in that year. Nakajima's design was designated Type 97 Carrier Attack Bomber Model 1, and the Mitsubishi the Type 97 Model 2—the respective short titles being B5N1 and B5M1.

There was little to choose between the performance of the two aircraft, but the Nakajima bomber was more advanced technically. It had a retractable main undercarriage and power-operated wing-folding—a feature not seen in Western carrier aircraft for some years after. Despite the extra weight of these fittings, the fully-loaded B5N weighed little more than that of the 'Val', in spite of an additional crew member, another 800lb of fuel, and more than double the war load. Maximum level speed, unladen, was only 10mph less than the dive-bomber's. Entering service in 1937, the B5M and B5N were five years ahead of any Western design in terms of both performance and efficiency. Both were code-named 'Kate' in 1942, although the Nakajima aircraft was the one most commonly encountered—the B5M being used only from shore bases.

The B5N's main anti-warship weapon was the Type 91 torpedo, a 45-knot 17.7in weapon which could be released at heights of up to 250ft and a speed of up to 280mph—higher and faster than any Allied air-launched torpedo. The warhead weight of 770lb (350kg) was also greater than that of its contemporaries—although at 1,760lb (800kg) the overall weight was not exceptional. A particular asset of the Type 91 torpedo was its ability to 'find' its correct running depth quickly after a steep angle of entry and a deep initial dive which would have sent any other torpedo straight to the bottom. 'Kate' tactics were to approach the target at about 12,000ft and begin a shallow dive at about 20 or 25 miles. By the time that they began to level out, within two miles of the target, they were travelling almost as fast as the maximum low-altitude speed of the defending fighters, and over 100mph faster than any other carrier-borne torpedo-bomber at the same stage of an attack. Attacking from two or more sectors, at low level, with dive-bombers coming down simultaneously at steep angles, the 'Kates' split the defenses—guns and fighters alike. Only the most experienced defensive formation could defeat such an attack.

A Nakajima B5N2, Navy Type 97 Carrier Attack Bomber Model 12, taking off from a Japanese carrier. The smaller cowling of the Nakajima Sakae II engine allowed better pilot vision. Armament was the Type 91 17.7in torpedo.

'Kate' was also intended for use as a level bomber. The observer/navigator aimed the bombs, using a simple sight—the 'Small Bombing Telescope No 4'. This device was adapted from the German Loetz sight and was able to make allowance for target movement as well as wind speed and direction. The 'Lead Bomber' technique was used—one experienced observer in the leading aircraft of a formation aiming and the remaining aircraft releasing bombs when his were seen to fall. 'Kate' could carry either a single 1,725lb bomb or a number of smaller bombs, often one 554lb and six 132lb bombs. These were all carried in tandem on a single beam carrier under the fuselage. The radio operator/gunner was provided with a Type 92 7.7mm machine-gun for rear defense.

In 1941, a more powerful engine was installed in the B5N, giving the plane an improved take-off performance and raising the maximum speed to 235mph at 10,000ft. The more powerful engine was also 'thirstier'. This reduced the maximum striking radius from 300 miles to 250 miles. This new model was designated B5N2. Most of the carrier units had been re-equipped with the newest 'Kate' by the beginning of December 1941.

At the time of the Japanese attack on Pearl Harbor, on 7 December 1941, there were 162 'Kates' and 135 'Vals' operational aboard seven carriers. The small *Ryujo*, in the Philippines area, had 18 'Kates' but no 'Vals'. Her deck was too short for the dive-bombers' somewhat long take-off run.

Of the six carriers involved in the 'Hawaiian Operation' *Akagi, Kaga, Hiryu* and *Soryu* were selected for the high-priority targets. Their aircrews were all highly experienced. These targets were the US Pacific Fleet warships docked at Pearl Harbor. The main brunt of the attack was to be delivered by 'Kates'. Forty of these were armed with Type 91 torpedoes modified for release in shallow water by the addition of a wooden 'air tail'. This ensured a shallow angle

JAPANESE BOMBS

Designation	Weight (lb)	Penetration (ins)
Type 97 No 6 *Land Bomb*	133	8 RC
Type 99 No 6 *Ordinary Bomb*	138	1 AP
Type 98 No 25 *Land Bomb*	538	15 RC
Type 99 No 25 *Ordinary Bomb*	554	2 AP
Type 99 No 80 *Mark 5 Bomb*	1,725	6 AP
Type 98 No 7 *Incendiary Bomb*	145	0.5 AP

(*AP* = armor plate; *RC* = reinforced concrete)

Note: *the 'Land' designation was the Japanese equivalent of the Allied 'Medium Capacity', with a filling case weight ratio of about 40:60; the 'Ordinary' bombs were the equivalent of 'Semi Armor-Piercing', with a 25% explosive filling. The Type 99 No 80 bomb was carried by 'Kate' and had only 3% explosive filling.*

of entry into the water. Another 50 bombers were each armed with a 1,725lb Type 99 No. 80 bomb. This bomb was a 16in armor-piercing naval shell adapted for use in the air by the addition of stabilizing fins and suspension lugs. *Shokaku* and *Zuikaku* did not enter service in time for their newly-formed air groups to take part in the special training for the attack. Their 'Kates' and 'Vals' were given the task of neutralizing the Oahu Island airfields with 538lb and 132lb medium-capacity bombs.

The first wave of the attack caught the defenses off-guard and despite the failure to explode of a sizeable proportion of torpedoes and armor-piercing bombs, seven battleships and five other ships were sunk or seriously damaged. The 81 'Vals' in the second wave sank or damaged a further eight ships. The bombers which attacked the airfields destroyed or crippled 177 US Navy, Marine Corps and Army Air Force aircraft on the six island airfields. This for

Japanese Navy

▷ A mixture of nine Zeros and 18 Vals, running-up on the deck of the Akagi before the launch of the second strike at Pearl Harbor. The 36,500-ton Akagi led the Strike Force, which was commanded by Vice-Admiral C. Nagumo. The carrier was eventually sunk by scuttling off Midway on 5 June 1942. Japanese aviation losses at Pearl Harbor were 29 aircraft out of the 350 that went into that successful attack. The Akagi ('Red Castle') had room for 66 combat aircraft and 25 spare. In the Midway action she carried 21 of each aircraft type. Her naval air officers were Japan's best; Cdr. Fuchida senior air wing officer in the Strike Force led the first wave at Pearl Harbor, Lt. Cdr. Murata led its torpedo Kates, Lt. Cdr. Itayu the fighter escort and Lt. Shindo the second wave's. These were the men who urged a third attack on Pearl, one which might have found the carrier USS Enterprise then 200 miles south of Oahu.

▷ A belly view of the B5N2 Kate, showing the offset 1,764lb (800kg) torpedo. There were 144 Kates at Pearl Harbor during the attack. This aircraft's performance surpassed the US Douglas Devastator.

Airview

the loss of one 'Val'! The harbor defenses had rallied quickly and five 'Kates' and 15 'Vals' were shot down. Also, nine 'Zero' fighters were lost in action around the island. The high proportion of dive-bomber losses reflected the extreme vulnerability of the 'Val'.

In the Philippines, Ryujo's 'Kates' were used as level bombers, attacking targets on land and sea. They were not spectacularly successful against shipping, but the possession of a carrier gave the Japanese a tremendous advantage over the Allied fleets in the East Indies area.

After operations in support of Japanese landings at Rabaul and on Ambon Island, Akagi, Kaga, Hiryu and Soryu arrived in the Indian Ocean to assist in the Java campaign. They sealed off the island from Allied reinforcements from

or evacuation to Australia and India. The cruise began with a devastating raid on Darwin, Northern Australia. Here the 'Vals' sank 11 ships and the level-bombing 'Kates' all but obliterated the military installations and stores dumps ashore. The only aircraft to be lost out of the 188 which attacked was a 'Val'—shot down by USAF Curtiss P-40 fighters. This raid, on 19 February 1942, was followed by two weeks of searches and attacks which accounted for another 12 ships sunk and six damaged at sea. Twenty more were sunk in Tjilitjap harbor on 5 March. To the north of Java, Ryujo's bombers sank an American destroyer.

The first real check came a month later, when Akagi, Hiryu, Soryu, Shokaku and Zuikaku attacked Colombo, Ceylon. Thirty-six 'Vals' and 53 level-bombing 'Kates' were

NAKAJIMA B5N2 'KATE'

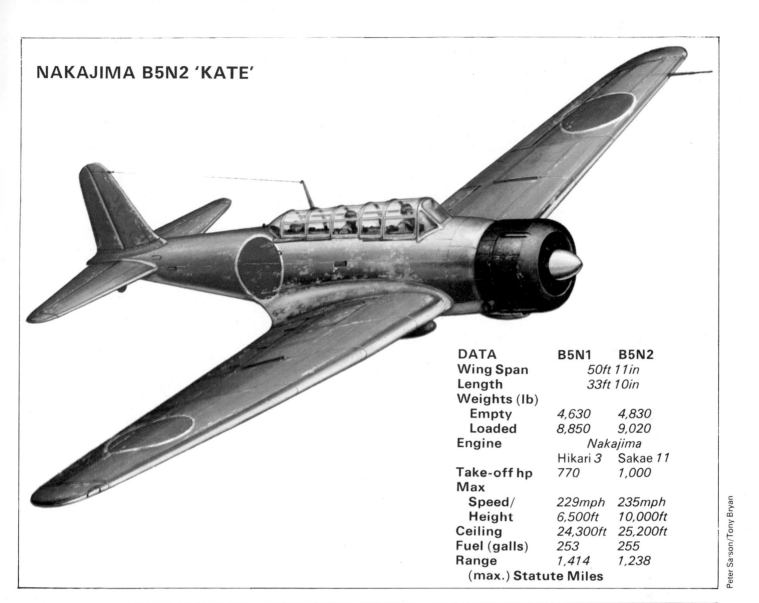

DATA	B5N1	B5N2
Wing Span	50ft 11in	
Length	33ft 10in	
Weights (lb)		
Empty	4,630	4,830
Loaded	8,850	9,020
Engine	Nakajima	
	Hikari 3	Sakae 11
Take-off hp	770	1,000
Max		
Speed/	229mph	235mph
Height	6,500ft	10,000ft
Ceiling	24,300ft	25,200ft
Fuel (galls)	253	255
Range	1,414	1,238
(max.) Statute Miles		

Peter Sarson/Tony Bryan

U.S. Navy

A Kate, all power on, during take-off with a torpedo. All three cockpit canopies are wide open to give the three-man crew air. A Japanese caption to this photograph says rocket-assisted take-off was used here.

intercepted by RAF and Navy fighters. Although no 'Kates' were shot down their concentration was upset and they sank only two ships and damaged three more out of the 34 ships in the harbor. The 'Vals', from *Shokaku* and *Zuikaku*, lost six of their number over the airfields but claimed four out of the 16 British fighters to be lost.

Shortly afterwards, 53 'Vals' took off from *Akagi*, *Hiryu* and *Soryu* to attack the British heavy cruisers *Cornwall* and *Dorsetshire,* to the south of Ceylon. The dive-bombers sank the cruisers in 19 minutes. Only one 'Val' was lost. These victims were the first major warships to be sunk in the open sea by Japanese carrier aircraft.

Four days later, on 9 April, 91 'Kates' bombed Trincomalee —the main naval base on Ceylon. Twenty-two British fighters intercepted the bombers, but the 'Kates' could take punishment. Although 12 were hit only two failed to return to their carriers. As off Colombo, however, the main honors of the day went to the 'Vals'. The small RN carrier HMS *Hermes*, without aircraft on board, was spotted, together with four other naval vessels and a hospital ship, to the south of Trincomalee. No fewer than 85 'Vals' from all five carriers took part in the attack. Nine out of ten aircraft scored hits—sinking the legitimate targets but respecting the hospital ship. Four of *Soryu's* 18 dive-bombers were shot down by Royal Navy Fulmar fighters which arrived as the ships were sinking. But the other 'Vals' turned on the fighters and shot two down. *Hermes* had been virtually defenseless, but to 'Val' goes the honor of sinking the first carrier to succumb to air attack alone.

While the 'Kates' from the big carriers were not enjoying much success, *Ryujo's* 16 aircraft were usefully employed in the Bay of Bengal—hunting down merchant shipping fleeing from Ceylon. On 5 and 6 April, 11 ships were sunk and two damaged by the 'Kates', which suffered no loss.

Price of the Lexington

Not until early May 1942 did the Japanese and American carriers meet in battle—in a series of engagements known as the Battle of the Coral Sea. The lack of experience of *Shokaku's* and *Zuikaku's* aircrew in shipping strike work was displayed on 7 May, when no fewer than 60 bomber sorties were needed to sink an oiler and a destroyer. They were identified by a carrier reconnaissance aircraft as a carrier and a light cruiser. This action cost the carriers one 'Val', and that evening 23 out of 27 'Kates' and 'Vals' which took off in search of *Yorktown* and *Lexington* failed to return—10 as the result of combat with the Americans and the others from accidents. The attack on 8 May, which resulted in the loss of *Lexington*, compensated for the previous evening's failure—but at a high price. At least 20 of the dive and torpedo-bombers were shot down, most during the get-away.

The main striking force for the Midway operation in early June 1942 was provided by the 'first team' of *Akagi*, *Kaga*, *Hiryu* and *Soryu,* with 90 'Vals' and 78 'Kates'. Involved in the diversionary strikes on the Aleutian Islands were *Ryujo*, with 18 'Kates' and the new *Junyo*, with the same number of 'Vals'. Another 19 torpedo-bombers were aboard *Zuiho* and *Hosho*, supporting the battle squadrons. Neither America nor Japan derived much benefit from the Aleutian raids.

The Battle of Midway began on 4 June 1942 with a strike against the island by 72 'Kates' and 'Vals'. They were launched before the Japanese learned that they were opposed by carriers. When the strike returned, less six

bombers shot down and as many damaged, there was indecision as to whether to attack the just-reported American fleet, or to revisit the Midway airfield.

The Douglas Devastator and Dauntless attacks from *Yorktown*, *Enterprise* and *Hornet* took place before any aircraft could be launched for either task. The American dive-bombers inflicted fatal damage on three carriers— leaving only *Hiryu* unscathed. She launched all 18 of her 'Vals' as soon as possible, and followed up two-and-a-half hours later with nine of her 'Kates' and one from *Akagi*. Seven or eight of the dive-bombers managed to erode the American fighter patrols and scored three hits on *Yorktown*. These hits were costly. Only three 'Vals' returned to *Hiryu*. The 'Kates' broke through as well and scored one torpedo hit—at the cost of five of their number. *Hiryu* was then savaged by Dauntless dive-bombers which pounded her to a blazing hulk. *Yorktown*, limping though she was, would probably have survived had she not been spotted and torpedoed by a submarine.

The US Marines invaded Guadalcanal Island on 7 August 1942. Six months of bitter fighting followed in which both sides suffered heavy air and naval losses—both in day-to-day fighting as well as 'set-piece' battles. For torpedo attacks and level bombing, the Japanese used the Mitsubishi 'Betty' twin-engined bombers based at Rabaul, so that 'Kate' was not employed very much during the campaign. The 27 'Vals' of the 33rd Air Group, which had taken part in the Java campaign, were flown from an airfield on Buka Island. The Guadacanal area, however, was at the extreme limit of their radius of action. In their first attack, on 8 August, 14 out of 18 were lost—several simply ran out of fuel. After this, the dive-bombers were not used for regular raids but were held in reserve for special operations.

There were two carrier battles off Guadalcanal—the Battle of the Eastern Solomons on 24 August and Santa Cruz (see 'War Monthly' issue 13) on 26 October 1942. In the first, 38 'Vals' from *Shokaku* and *Zuikaku* damaged *Enterprise*, but lost 18, while the 'Kates' enjoyed no success at all. At Santa Cruz, the survivors of the Pearl Harbor veterans scored their last success—sinking the carrier *Hornet* with torpedoes and bombs, and damaging *Enterprise*, a battleship and a light cruiser by bombing. Two 'unofficial *kamikaze*' attacks were made, one by a 'Kate' on a destroyer, and the other by a 'Val' on *Hornet*. The true *kamikaze* suicide group was not then formed. Both aircraft hit their marks. The cost was again heavy. At least 60 Japanese attack-aircraft were shot down. At the time of the Battle of Guadalcanal, during the second week in November 1942, the only Japanese bombers at sea were the 27 'Vals' and 18 'Kates' aboard *Junyo* and *Hiyo*. *Hiyo* lost 12 dive-bombers in an attempt to attack shipping off Guadalcanal during the battle.

A more powerful variant of 'Val' entered service in September 1942 and was in action at Santa Cruz. This was the D3A2, fitted with a 1,200hp engine. Fuel capacity had been raised from 160 gallons to 237 gallons. The new aircraft had a top speed of 267mph at 20,000ft and a radius of action of 330 miles. The maximum bomb-load was not increased and crew or fuel protection was not incorporated.

The Solomons island campaign continued to sap Japanese naval air strength throughout 1943. The rebuilt carrier air groups disembarked at Rabaul in early April. 'Vals' took part in two strikes in the area, losing 15 out of the 89 planes involved and sinking five ships. The carrier aircraft returned to their ships later in the month, leaving the shore-based

◁ By the use of two dive-bombers and two torpedo-bombers, the AA defenses of a warship can be swamped. The two dive-bombers would attack from a height and each aim for one end of the ship; the two low torpedo-bombers would come in from port and starboard. This gave the ship little room for the standard maneuver to avoid torpedo attack, which was to steer towards the torpedo tracks, thus showing a more narrow profile.

◁ In a huge explosion, the doomed USS Lexington's magazines erupt. Kates and Vals pounced on the US carrier, which was hit by torpedoes and bombs.

▽ A remarkable photograph taken from the deck of a US carrier, the Yorktown. The AA defenses of the ship poured shells into the path of this attacking Japanese plane. It needed just one piece of shrapnel, or one bullet from an MG to hit the aircraft's unprotected fuel tanks. This was the result: before the pilot had time to release his torpedo the plane burst into flames and went out of control.

'Vals'—joined later by 'Kates'—to fight the advancing Allied forces. These aircraft suffered heavily for few rewards. They lost 209 of their number between May and November 1943. The carrier air groups returned in November, this time to strike at the ships supporting the landings on Bougainville Island. American carrier air superiority was by now almost total. When 27 'Vals' and 14 'Kates' tried to attack a carrier force near Rabaul, the Hellcats and Corsairs destroyed all the torpedo-bombers and 17 dive-bombers.

'Kate' was clearly unable to deliver a successful daylight attack on warships. But she was to score two more successes when used for night attacks. On 4 December, 'Kates' based in the Marshalls Islands joined 'Betties' in a series of day and night torpedo attacks on an American carrier striking force. The new Lexington was torpedoed by a 'Kate' shortly before midnight and had to be withdrawn for extensive repairs. Seventeen 'Kates' and 18 'Betties' were sacrificed for this one hit.

On 17 and 18 February 1944, aircraft from nine fast carriers struck at Truk Atoll, the main Japanese advanced base in the SW Pacific. Over 250 Japanese aircraft were destroyed and damaged in the air and on the ground. Six 'Kates' struck back after dark on the 17th, slipping past a radar-equipped night-fighter and inflicting a hit on Intrepid—putting her out of action for months.

The last major carrier battle took place on 19 and 20 June 1944, west of the Marianas. Nine Japanese carriers took part, but only four had 'Vals' and 'Kates' as principal types while the two large carriers Shokaku and Taiho had seven between them. Junyo and Hiyo were unable to operate the new Yokosuka 'Judy' dive-bombers, which had an even longer take-off run than 'Val'. Therefore, she retained 27 of the older dive-bombers, while the smaller converted carriers operated 'Zero' fighter-bombers. The new torpedo-bomber embarked in seven carriers, was the Nakajima B6N2 'Jill', but the smallest ships, Chitose and Chiyoda, had to be armed with the lighter 'Kates'. There were nine aboard each ship.

On 19 June, the 'Kates' were used as scouts, shadowing the vast American carrier force. Ten were lost to the defending Hellcats. The 'Vals' from Junyo and Hiyo never got close to the enemy and 20 were shot down—out-dated aircraft pitted against a modern defensive system.

After 'The Great Marianas Turkey Shoot' the useful life of both 'Kate' and 'Val' was over as carrier-based strike aircraft, but other jobs were found for them. American submarine activity was steadily strangling the Japanese war economy by inflicting savage losses on shipping between the Home Islands, China and SE Asia. 'Kate' was therefore adapted for anti-submarine warfare by the fitting of 'Model 6 Airborne Radar': This had a range of about eight miles against a surfaced submarine. From mid-1944, a Magnetic Anomaly Detector was added, with a range of 450ft against a submerged submarine. Flying from shore bases in Kyushu, Formosa and mainland China, as well as from the escort carriers Kaiyo, Shinyo, Taiyo and Unyo, 'Kates' of Nakajima and Mitsubishi design were responsible for a few 'kills'. It was ironic, however, that of the carriers, three were sunk by submarine attacks, in August, September, and November 1944, only Kaiyo survived until August 1945.

The final role for the two aircraft was suicide attack. Introduced in October 1944 as an officially recognized method of war, it was initially delivered by modern aircraft, such as the 'Zero' fighter and 'Judy' dive-bomber. But on 13 December 1944 a 'Val' inflicted heavy damage and serious casualties on USS Nashville. She was carrying amphibious forces headquarters staff to the Mindoro Island invasion. The first sinking by a kamikaze 'Val' was that of the tanker Porcupine, off Mindoro on 30 December. Further damage was inflicted during the Lingayen Gulf invasion of Luzon Island in January 1945, and the large-scale use of 'Vals' during April and May off Okinawa resulted in the sinking of two destroyers and the damaging of a dozen assorted vessels.

The 'Kates' of the anti-submarine units were also pressed into service for suicide operations in May 1945, armed with a single 1,775lb medium-capacity bomb. They achieved no significant success. They were only used in small numbers, and only 25 were claimed shot down by American carrier fighters. Compare this with 150 'Vals' shot by down British and American aircraft off Okinawa. A 'Val' scored the last kamikaze hit of the war—damaging the destroyer USS Borie off Japan on 9 August.

In combination, the Nakajima B5N 'Kate' and Aichi D3A 'Val' were responsible for sinking more Allied shipping than any other air attack team. Always vulnerable to heavy losses against strong opposition, their success declined sharply from the autumn of 1942 when the last of the experienced aircrews perished in the struggle for Guadalcanal. The obsolescence of the aircraft and the inexperience of the crews after Guadalcanal led to increasingly heavy losses for meagre rewards. By June 1944, the successes at Pearl Harbor, Darwin and Java were but a memory. **David Brown**

Kates in the level bomber role. They are carrying the Type 99 No. 80 MK 5 bomb, a 1,759lb conversion of a 16in naval shell with a 3% explosive filling giving 6in of armor penetration. USS Arizona was blown up by them at Pearl Harbor.

YAMATO AND MUSASHI

The world's greatest battleships were also Japan's doomed giants

U.S. Navy

A violent sea is tamed by the mightiest battleship in the Imperial Japanese Navy. The 64,000-ton Yamato *was, along with* Musashi, *built to be unsinkable. Her 23,500 tons of armor could withstand direct hits which would sink lesser craft.*

'These battleships will be as useful in modern warfare as a *samurai* sword,' predicted Admiral Isoroku Yamamoto, C-in-C, of Japan's Combined Fleet. He was talking about *Yamato* and *Musashi*, the largest and most powerful battleships ever built. Yet on 16 December 1941, days after Pearl Harbor and sinking the *Prince of Wales* and *Repulse*—the first ever capital ships sunk *at sea* by air attack—the Imperial Japanese Navy took delivery of the 64,000-ton *Yamato*. She was already obsolescent.

The first *Yamato*-class designs envisaged ships 965ft overall with a standard 69,500-ton displacement. By July 1936, the *22nd* design since the project's beginning in 1934, plans were for a 64,000-ton ship 860ft long. Two pairs of propellors, one steam-turbine driven, the other diesel powered, would give the reduced 27-knot requirement. The heavier diesels were compensated for by lower fuel consumption. However, trouble with experimental diesels led to only steam-turbines being adopted for the new battleships. The 23rd and final design was finished in March 1937, and *Yamato's* keel laid at Kure Navy Yard on 4 November. Advance preparations included deepening the building dock; providing a crane able to lift single 100-ton armor plates; and erecting 20ft high fences, protective roofing and rope screens to hide construction. Similar precautions were taken at the Mitsubishi Company's Nagasaki yard where the keel of *Musashi* was laid on 29 March 1938. Her launching weight of 35,737 tons (surpassed only by the liner *Queen Mary*) necessitated a 13ft-wide slipway, the world's largest. The keel of a third vessel, *Shinano*, converted to an aircraft carrier while building, was laid in Yokosuka Navy Yard on 4 May 1940. These were the only ships of the class to be launched: a fourth, hull number *111*, was scrapped at Kure in December 1941 when about 30 per cent complete. Orders for hulls *797*, *798* and *799* (two planned to mount 6 x 20in guns) were cancelled in 1942.

A striking feature of *Yamato* (statistics also apply to *Musashi*) was the great width of her beam—127ft 8in. There was a need for the shallowest possible draught in Japan's coastal waters. The ship's vital parts had to be packed into the smallest space to have maximum armor protection without exceeding the designed displacement. Fully loaded, displacing 72,809 tons, *Yamato* had the relatively shallow mean draught of 35ft 6in. Vital machinery was crammed into a length representing only 53.5 per cent of her total waterline; achieved by arranging the 12 x 13,500hp boilers in four rows of three, each headed by and linked to one of the four turbines. This area was protected by 16in plates of Vickers armor, the largest weighing 70 tons. Side armor extended all the way from the $7\frac{3}{4}$in armored deck down to the bottom hull plates. Sloping slightly outwards to minimise shell impact, they formed a supposed impregnable bulkhead within a comparatively lightly armored torpedo-bulge. Compartments housing main and auxiliary steering gear—the ship had two rudders, provision of a second fairly late in building perhaps influenced by the fate of the German *Bismarck* in May 1941—were similarly protected. The 16in plates could withstand an 18in shell hit from 13-18 mile ranges. The $7\frac{3}{4}$in deck was proof against anything under a 2,200lb armor-piercing bomb dropped from 10,000ft. The heaviest armor of all, 22in front plates on the main gun turrets, could withstand an 18in shell travelling at 550ft per second. Some of the heaviest side armor plates also served as longitudinal hull strength members. Except on longitudinal members and other vital lower parts, more weight was saved by electric welding.

Japan spent an estimated £4 million on increasing steel production and developing hardening processes to make *Yamato* truly 'unsinkable'. Even lesser protection was impressive. Upper deck $1\frac{1}{2}$in-$1\frac{7}{8}$in armor could withstand a 500lb bomb. Two feet below the armored deck, a splinter-proof $\frac{1}{4}$in Ducol steel screen shielded crewmen. Magazine floors were given 2in-3in plating to absorb torpedo or mine explosions beneath the ship's double bottom. The funnel

19

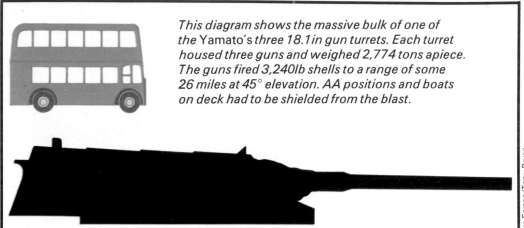

This diagram shows the massive bulk of one of the Yamato's three 18.1in gun turrets. Each turret housed three guns and weighed 2,774 tons apiece. The guns fired 3,240lb shells to a range of some 26 miles at 45° elevation. AA positions and boats on deck had to be shielded from the blast.

△ 24 October 1944. Musashi *was attacked by the full weight of American naval air power. For 6½ hours—from 1026 to 1650—* Musashi's *decks were strafed and shelled.*
△ ▷ *At 1715 the battle flag was lowered and the order 'Abandon ship!' given. Finally, down at the bows, she rolled to port and sank at 1925. (Inset) Vice Admiral Takeo Kurita commander of the 1st Striking Force.*

Peter Sarson/Tony Bryan

was shielded by specially designed *perforated* 15in plates. The total 23,500 tons of armor protection on Yamato was about 34 per cent of her total tonnage: she and *Musashi* were the most heavily armored ships ever built.

So Yamato could take punishment, and she could most certainly hand it out. Her 18in guns threw 3,240lb shells (1,000lb heavier than 16in shells) 25 miles. The British light battlecruiser *Furious* (1917) had been designed to mount two 18in, but she was converted into an aircraft carrier and her big guns remounted singly in two monitors, sold by 1927. The Japanese giants mounted 9 x 18in; some idea of the weight problem can be gained by comparing these guns with the 16in of *Nagato*. The smaller battleship's four twin turrets totalled 6,827 tons; *Yamato's* triple turrets each weighed 2,774 tons. The guns and their mountings were cast at Kure, and a specially built ship transported *Musashi's* to Nagasaki. The muzzle blast of the triple-mounted 18in barrels (up to 16ft away) was six times the 'danger point' at which vulnerable installations would be badly damaged and men knocked unconscious. Boats and fittings on the main deck had to be specially protected, while all AA positions there had to be shielded.

In spite of a massive bulbous bow—experiments with 50 ship models in a special 805ft testing tank had shown that this minimised hull resistance and increased engine efficiency—Yamato was a handsome ship with good handling qualities—a comparatively small turning circle and a freedom from excessive heel. Most Japanese battleship foremasts had a clumsy 'pagoda' outline but *Yamato's* was a streamlined cylindrical tower surmounted by triple 49ft rangefinders and the main armament director. A Type 21 air/surface radar was later mounted atop the rangefinders.

She was a good ship to sail in, with air-conditioned officers' cabins and ample crew quarters designed for a 2,200 complement, but more often housing a war-time 2,500. In comfort, Yamato was reckoned inferior to *Musashi* which sailors nicknamed 'The Palace'.

Both ships were launched as secretly as they had been built. Men working on *Musashi* were not allowed to leave Nagasaki Yard before the launch; they worked a final 24-hour shift to ready her, while troops sealed off the Yard from Nagasaki city. The Imperial Navy's officers, like most contemporary naval officers, still saw battleships as the major striking force, with carriers in a secondary role.

On 12 February 1942, Yamamoto hoisted his flag in *Yamato*, the new flagship of his *Rengo Kantai* (Combined Fleet). As she lay at Hashira anchorage in Hiroshima Bay, the C-in-C called senior officers aboard for four days' war-gaming to decide Japan's next move. The result was 'Plan A.F.', to capture Midway atoll, a move that Yamamoto hoped would lure the US Pacific Fleet out to battle—and destruction.

Yamamoto's 162 warships included 11 battleships and eight carriers. Admiral Chester W. Nimitz, US C-in-C Pacific, had 76 ships, '. . . three (aircraft carriers) are all that stand between the Japanese fleet and the American coastline'.

Thanks to the cracking of Japan's top-secret naval code, Nimitz was able to establish where and when the attack would come. Plan A.F.'s weaknesses did the rest. Yamamoto's mistake in positioning the main body, with flagship *Yamato* and six other battleships, 300 miles astern of the First Carrier Striking Force, was compounded by over-confidence that led to neglect of air and submarine recon-

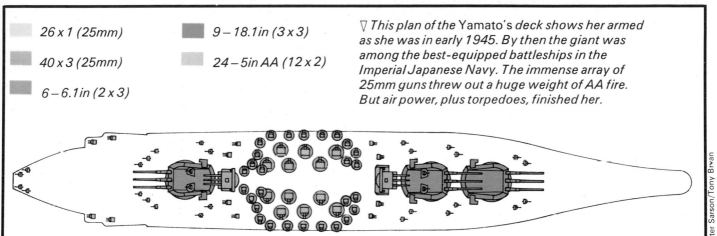

▨ 26 x 1 (25mm)	▨ 9 – 18.1in (3 x 3)
▨ 40 x 3 (25mm)	▨ 24 – 5in AA (12 x 2)
▨ 6 – 6.1in (2 x 3)	

▽ This plan of the Yamato's deck shows her armed as she was in early 1945. By then the giant was among the best-equipped battleships in the Imperial Japanese Navy. The immense array of 25mm guns threw out a huge weight of AA fire. But air power, plus torpedoes, finished her.

naissance. Nimitz's advance knowledge swiftly gave him a fairly clear picture and, from his HQ in Pearl Harbor, he exerted effective overall command—unlike Yamamoto, keeping radio silence in Yamato some 10 hours behind his carriers. Lacking radar, three carriers were surprised and sunk with planes jamming their decks. On Yamato some 30 minutes later, Yamamoto displayed unwonted emotion on hearing of the mortal damage inflicted. His reaction was to order the battleships on to Midway at full speed. In anti-submarine formation, zig-zagging at 20 knots, Yamato and her consorts entered thick fog. With most aboard tense for a collision, Yamamoto called a conference. Signals were sent ordering other units to rendezvous with Yamamoto for a night bombardment of Midway.

An error by Yamamoto, and wary American maneuvering, ruled out a night action, leaving the Japanese commander to consider the risk of a daylight attack without air support. The risk was too great. Shadowed by US aircraft, Yamamoto led his force back to Japan, spending the voyage in the seclusion of his great cabin aboard the battleship he must have despised even more deeply. Worse than the loss of four carriers was losing 250 aircraft with most of their trained crews. Yamamoto's bitterness can hardly have abated when the newly-completed Musashi joined the fleet on 5 August 1942, but at least he got the third and last 'super-ship', Shinano, converted to a heavy carrier.

Imperial Headquarters had not lost faith in the battleships. Late in August, Yamamoto's flag flew in Yamato as she headed a strong force bound for Truk atoll, from which the Navy was to support the Army's struggle for Guadalcanal in the Solomon Islands. Guadalcanal was lost by February 1943, when Musashi, having joined Yamato at Truk,

replaced her as flagship. At the end of April 1943, a small white box was carried aboard Musashi—the ashes of Adm. Yamamoto who had been shot down over Bougainville island. Both the great ships dropped anchor at Yokosuka on 21 May. Headed by the Emperor himself, naval officers trooped aboard to pay their last respects. On Yamato, they found a poem by the Admiral. It began: 'So many are dead, I cannot face the Emperor . . . soon I shall join the young dead soldiers'.

After a spell in dry dock at Kure, Yamato and Musashi joined the new C-in-C, Admiral Mineichi Koga, at Truk in the autumn. Yamato's first 'action' came late in December, as she prepared for Operation Ro, an assault on the central Solomons. As she entered Truk anchorage, a single torpedo from the submarine Skate struck her aft on the starboard hull, driving in the heavy side armor more than 3ft and buckling its brackets. Yamato shipped 3,000 tons of water and was not operational until April 1944. Meanwhile Musashi joined her on the casualty list. When heavy air attacks forced Koga to leave Truk for the Palau islands, Musashi sailed as his flagship. US carrier planes struck at Palau, while seven submarines ringed the islands to intercept ships flushed from cover. On 29 March, the submarine Tunny torpedoed Musashi's port bow, killing or wounding 18 men. Koga ordered her back to Japan and himself boarded an aircraft to disappear without trace en route for a new base.

Admiral Soemu Toyoda completed Koga's organization of the new 1st Fleet, remaining carriers were concentrated in Vice-Admiral Jisaburo Ozawa's 3rd Fleet and the battle-ships formed part of Vice-Admiral Takeo Kurita's 2nd Fleet. Vice-Admiral Matome Ugaki, commanding 1st Battleship

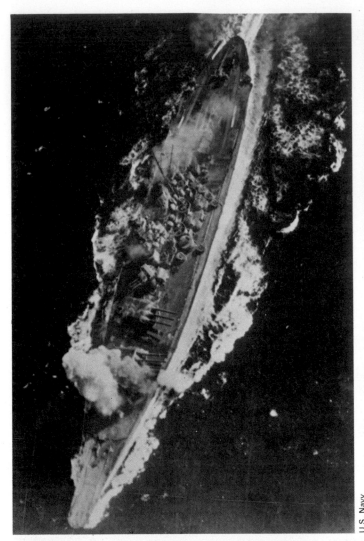

◁△ *A combat photograph showing, for the first time, the* Yamato *under attack by American air power in the Battle of Sibuyan Sea. On this occasion, the* Yamato *escaped destruction— thanks to her superb handling qualities.*

△ *19 March 1945.* Yamato *is attacked by planes from the American carrier* Hornet *in Kure Bay off Honshu Island. Here, her fine maneuverability was fully put to the test as she strove to avoid American bombs. But even the nimble* Yamato *could not elude all the bombs. She was severely damaged after several direct hits, only surviving because of her formidable armor.*

◁ *7 April 1945.* Yamato *under attack south of Kyushu. She sank at 1423.*

Division (*Yamato, Musashi, Nagato*), flew his flag in *Yamato*. His force made its base at Tawi-Tawi in the Sulu islands, off NE Borneo. In May-June 1944, Ugaki's battleships were ordered to take part in Operation *Kon*, to blast the newly-landed Allies off Biak island, NW of New Guinea, but were recalled into the Philippine Sea. Here Ozawa hoped to destroy the American fleet 'with one blow', but the blow was never struck and battleships played no part in the campaign which crippled Japanese naval airpower. Three carriers went down and close on 500 aircraft and their crews were lost in such actions as 'The Great Marianas Turkey Shoot' of 19 June. Soon the Philippines were threatened, while *Yamato* and *Musashi*, the *hashira* ('stay-at-home') fleet, as other ships' crews began to call them, were back in Japan.

For *Yamato* and *Musashi*, the build-up for the Philippines began in July 1944 when, after at last acquiring radar and radar-directed fire-control for their great guns, they went south for intensive training in the Lingga archipelago, south of Singapore. The battleships resumed their role as the main striking force; Japan's carriers could no longer spearhead a battle. North of Leyte Island, the carriers were to draw off American air cover and give battleships a chance against the vulnerable landing forces. On 18 October 1944, hearing of the initial landings in Leyte Gulf, Imperial Headquarters ordered Operation *Sho-1* (Victory) to begin. The two leviathans sailed from Lingga refuelling at Brunei among the three other battleships, 12 cruisers, and 15 destroyers of Kurita's 1st Striking Force.

Early on 23 October, NE of Palawan island, US submarines sank two of Kurita's heavy cruisers, one flying Kurita's flag. In the confusion of panic anti-submarine action, ten hours passed before Kurita could join Ugaki aboard *Yamato* and resume command; by then three US carrier task groups had Kurita under observation. Determined to rendezvous with two other squadrons in the Sulu Sea, Kurita pressed on without air cover, telling his staff: 'It would be shameful for the fleet to remain intact while our nation perishes . . . you must remember that miracles do happen.' But he would never keep his appointment—the other forces were annihilated in or fled from Surigao Strait on the night of 24-25 October—and no miracle would save *Musashi*, main target of American aircraft for the next five hours.

Bombs made little impression

At 1026, 12 Curtiss Helldiver bombers, 12 Grumman Avenger torpedo planes and 21 Grumman Hellcat fighters hit Kurita's force in Tablas Strait. The Japanese ships threw up a fierce barrage, knocking down two Avengers, but the Americans pressed home attacks on *Yamato* and *Musashi*. Bombs made little impression on their armored decks; torpedoes would prove more effective. During the first 20 minutes *Musashi* took four torpedoes on the port side and one to starboard. But now the design proved its intrinsic worth: *Musashi* stayed on course without apparent difficulty. A second 42-aircraft strike arrived around noon. Again *Musashi* bore the brunt, taking two bombs and two torpedoes, and began to show signs of slowing down. After a third strike by 68 aircraft at 1325, *Musashi's* speed dropped to about 20 knots. She had taken nine torpedoes: her starboard bow twisted into a huge scoop into which water was forced by the ship's own momentum. Yet counter-flooding kept her under way with only a slight list to port, while seven hits and some 15 near-misses from bombs did

little structural damage. *Yamato* took two more bombs without effect. Many of the attackers were launched as quickly as possible carrying only 500lb GP bombs.

Musashi plowed on, but now her crew knew she was in bad shape. The AA gunners were making poor practice, and Rear Admiral Toshihara Inoguchi at first refused to allow the 18in to fire *sanshiki-dan* ('case-shot', with a 'shotgun' scatter of 20mm incendiary projectiles, supposedly effective over several thousand yards against aircraft) for fear of barrel damage. By early afternoon, as *Musashi's* bow sank lower and she began to fall behind, it became obvious he must change his mind if she was to survive.

By 1500, after another 30-plane strike which *sanshiki-dan* did little to inhibit, *Musashi's* speed had dropped to 12 knots. Kurita, about to reverse course hoping to lose the attackers, ordered her to drop out of formation. Only one cruiser remained with the stricken giant when more than 100 aircraft struck in wave after wave from 1515.

Death blows from Hellcats

The death blows were dealt by 12 Hellcats, nine Helldivers with 1,000lb bombs and eight Avenger torpedo planes from *Enterprise*. They found *Musashi* well down by the bows, staggering along at 12 knots and leaving a broad wake of oil. As the Helldivers plunged, Hellcats hammered her decks with .5 machine-gun fire and 5in rockets. Eleven more bombs reduced the already battered upper works to twisted wreckage, and a low-level torpedo attack ripped out her heart—all eight pilots claimed hits. At 1650, when the planes turned away, *Musashi* was listing 15° to port, her bows under water, the forward turrets islands, and making six knots. Inoguchi, mortally wounded, wanted to beach her on Sibuyan, but she was now so far over that use of the rudder risked an immediate capsize. Calling his remaining officers together, Inoguchi gave his sword to a young ensign, giving another a letter asking the Emperor's forgiveness. At 1715 the battle-flag was lowered and given to a strong swimmer, as was the Emperor's portrait. 'Abandon ship' was ordered, but when *Musashi* rolled over to port and sank at 1925, Inoguchi, Captain Kenchika Kato, who had lashed himself to the compass binnacle, and 1,023 of her 2,400-strong crew were still aboard. The battleship had taken between 11 and 19 torpedoes and at least 17 direct bomb hits. Kurita's ships had only downed 30 of their tormentors.

Although *Musashi's* sacrifice had saved all but one of Kurita's 28 other ships from significant damage, his reversal of course lent weight to American pilots' reports that he was retreating with heavy losses. The aircrews cannot fairly be blamed for an over-optimistic verdict, or for concentrating on a single prestige ship. But Admiral William F. 'Bull' Halsey would not escape criticism: at 1950, accepting that Kurita was finished, he led 15 fleet carriers and eight modern battleships on a chase after Ozawa. This left San Bernardino Strait unguarded, with only older battleships and light carriers to cover the landings.

At 0645 on 25 October, having reversed course again and cleared San Bernardino Strait at night, Kurita made contact with the six escort carriers, three destroyers and four destroyer-escorts of Rear Admiral Clifton A. F. Sprague's 'Taffy 3' group. But instead of sending light cruisers and destroyers to make torpedo attacks, while bringing his big ships out of their circular AA formation, the excited and combat-weary Kurita ordered 'General Chase'. At 0659, *Yamato's* great guns spoke in anger for the first time, at a range of 20 miles.

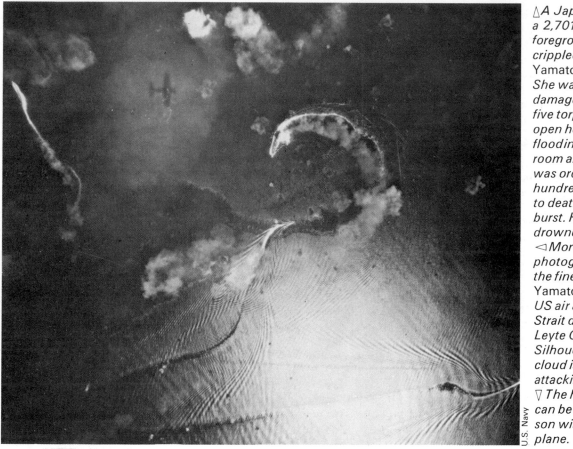

△ *A Japanese destroyer, a 2,701-ton Type B in the foreground, circles the crippled and sinking* Yamato *on 7 April 1945. She was already badly damaged when at least five torpedoes smashed open her port side. The flooding of the engine room and boiler rooms was ordered. Several hundred men were scalded to death as the boilers burst. Hundreds more drowned when she sank.*
◁ *More combat photography shows clearly the fine maneuverability of* Yamato. *Here she is under US air attack off Tablas Strait during the battle of Leyte Gulf in October 1944. Silhouetted against thin cloud is one of the many attacking aircraft.*
▽ *The huge bulk of* Yamato *can be gauged by comparison with the Aichi floatplane.*

In spite of confusion among Kurita's ships, gunnery was excellent. As Sprague ordered his carriers to make smoke and run, sending out a 'May Day' call in clear language, multi-colored marker dyes from the Japanese shells blossomed near his vulnerable 'flat-tops'. A rain squall hid them for 10 precious minutes as they worked up speed to launch aircraft—Japanese radar proving inadequate for blind firing, but at 0716 the rain lifted. Desperate to buy time, Sprague's seven destroyers raced towards a Japanese battle line that outgunned them by more than forty to one, weaving between shell splashes and closed to under 10,000 yards before launching torpedoes. The cruiser *Kumano* took crippling hits, while the *Heermann* sent a torpedo spread at *Yamato*.

Swinging away, the Japanese giant found herself between torpedo tracks heading for her stern. She was forced to run at full speed out of the action for 10 minutes. By 0742, when the destroyers launched a second attack, Sprague's planes were up, swarming to the attack, making 'dry' runs when their loads were expended. Such determination seemed to confirm Kurita in his mistaken belief that he was engaging the heavy carriers of Halsey's fleet. At 0915, when three US destroyers were gone, one carrier ablaze, and Japanese cruisers within 10,000 yards of the remainder, Kurita ordered the battle to be broken off. *Yamato* and her consorts fled back to Brunei, harassed all the way, although two more bomb hits did no more significant damage than the 104 rounds of 18in she had expended against Sprague's ships. Heavy air attacks soon forced a withdrawal from Brunei; on 23 November 1944, *Yamato* came home to Japan. She would only once more venture outside the Inland Sea, where aircraft of Task Force 58 inflicted minor damage on her during a raid on 19 March 1945.

Meanwhile the third and last *Yamato*-class ship had begun and ended a career as inglorious as any in naval history. *Shinano* mounted a formidable AA battery of 16 x 5in guns, 145 x 25mm and 336 x 5in rocket launchers, and with her multiplicity of watertight compartments she was deemed unsinkable. But when she sailed at 1800 on 29 November 1944, rushed away from Yokosuka under threat of air raids, her watertight doors lacked gaskets, open channels awaiting piping ran between her compartments, steam pumps had not been fitted and hand pumps were few.

The submarine *Archerfish's* radar picked up *Shinano* and her three destroyers at 2048 as they moved down the coast. Surfacing, the submarine took up a 20-knot chase in the darkness, able to keep in touch only because the ships zig-zagged—as an anti-submarine measure! At 0300 on 30 November, a sharp change of course by *Shinano* made her a perfect target, broadside on to *Archerfish* at 1,400 yards. Commander Joseph Enright fired a full spread of six 21in torpedoes at 0310. At least four struck the huge carrier. But *Musashi's* ordeal had shown what punishment the *Yamato*-class could take, and although he could easily have made harbor, or at worst beached his ship, Captain Toshio Abe ordered course to be held at 20 knots. For seven hours water poured in, flooding 'watertight' compartments and springing badly welded hull members. Too late, Abe realized the full peril. At 1055, *Shinano* rolled over to starboard and sank stern first, taking down the Captain and 500 of his 1,400-strong crew. Her life as an operational warship had lasted only 17 hours.

Early in 1945, the Imperial Navy's surviving warships swung at anchor in the Inland Sea, lacking fuel or air cover for effective sorties. At Imperial Headquarters, the Army angrily demanded that the Navy, in particular *Yamato*—'that floating hotel for idle, inept admirals'—match the self-sacrifice of *kamikaze* flyers, submariners and the island garrisons fighting to the last man.

When the Americans cornered the garrison of Okinawa, Adm. Toyoda, could resist no longer. He must throw away as many ships as could still be fuelled, *Yamato* among them, in an empty gesture to satisfy national honor and as an inspiration to the civilian millions soon to be called upon to make the final suicidal stand on the beaches of the home-land. On 5 April 1945, he issued orders for Operation *Ten-Go*. Vice-Admiral Seiichi Ito's 'Special Sea Attack Force' (*Yamato*, the light cruiser *Yahagi* and eight destroyers) was (in Toyoda's words) to make 'the most tragic and heroic attack of the war'. In support of a massive *kamikaze* effort, the ships were to sail for Okinawa; draw off air cover from the landing areas; smash through the US Navy's screen; run aground and as armored citadels hammer enemy-occupied areas until ammunition was exhausted. Then their crews were to go ashore and fight to the death.

With fuel for a one-way trip and magazines crammed with more than 1,000 rounds of 18in shells. *Yamato* sailed from Tokuyama at 1500 hours on 6 April 1945. Around 1800, shortly before clearing Bungo Strait, while the crew answered a patriotic exhortation from Ariga with *banzai* for the Emperor, US submarines *Hackleback* and *Threadfin* sighted the squadron. Evading destroyer attack, they flashed

Peter Sarson/Tony Bryan

a warning south. Three carrier task groups moved northeast from Okinawa, with orders a for dawn reconnaissance.

At 0832 on 7 April, a scout plane picked up *Yamato* and her escort south of Kyushu, heading SW at 22 knots. Ordering battleships to stand ready for any eventuality north of Okinawa, Admiral Raymond A. Spruance told Vice-Admiral Marc A. Mitscher: 'You take them'. Between 1000 and 1100, a dozen carriers from his Task Force 58 flew off 386 aircraft: 180 Hellcat and Corsair fighters, each carrying three 500lb bombs; 131 Avenger torpedo planes; and 75 Helldivers, each with one semi-armor-piercing or general purpose 1,000lb bomb and two 250-pounders.

Two Martin Mariner flying boats sighted Ito's ships at 1014, just as he swung south with 300 miles to go. Now they shadowed the small fleet, screened from *Yamato's* 18in *sanshiki-dan* by low cloud and frequent showers, while they guided in the carrier planes. Apart from two seaplanes that remained unlaunched aboard *Yamato* and *Yahagi*, no Japanese aircraft were to be seen. At 1210, the destroyer *Asashimo*, which had dropped back with engine trouble, flashed a brief warning as around 100 aircraft found her. At 1220, *Yamato's* radar located the first attack wave 18 miles to port. At 1232, about 200 planes were in sight at 13 miles range. To many American flyers, groping their way through blinding rain, massive bursts of *sanshiki-dan* were the first indication of their target's proximity.

The first wave struck at 1241, as *Yamato* raced south at close on 30 knots, the eight escorts in diamond formation around her. With only 3,000ft cloud ceiling, the planes came down in small groups to make low-level attacks. *Yamato's* great guns soon fell silent; their blast made it impossible for gunners to operate her massed 25mm batteries, but a heavy barrage met the Americans. To little avail: by 1248 one destroyer had sunk, *Yahagi* was crippled and *Yamato* had taken two bombs amidships as well as a torpedo in the port bow. Two more torpedoes struck there minutes later, while bombs silenced more of the battleship's AA guns. But *Yamato*, taking water and listing slightly to port, was still full of fight when a strike of 120 planes arrived at 1300. In less than 15 minutes, five more torpedoes ripped open *Yamato's* port side, while bombs and machine-gun fire silenced almost every remaining gun. Soon the list to port

was too great for the damage-control tanks to correct. To bring his ship back on an even keel, Ariga ordered the flooding of the lowest starboard compartments, the engine and boiler rooms. Several hundred men drowned or were scalded to death at their posts as the sea rushed in. The cruiser *Yahagi* now sank after taking seven torpedoes and 12 bombs.

From 1400 onwards, aircraft from *Intrepid* and *Yorktown* closed in for the kill. *Yamato* lay over at 35°, creeping at 7 knots in a circle with rudder jammed hard aport and only one working pair of propellers. Few guns spoke from her shattered deck. All external and internal communications were severed. The sick bay was gutted, doctors, orderlies and patients all dead. Coming in on the starboard side at the head of six Avengers from *Yorktown*, Lieutenant Thomas Stetson saw that *Yamato's* hull lay exposed beneath the armored belt. At least five of the Avengers' torpedoes ran straight. The last struck home at 1417.

Aboard the doomed battleship, Adm. Ito ordered the crew away at around 1405, shaking hands with his officers before retiring to his cabin to face death alone. Ariga, like Kato in *Musashi*, saw to the safety of the Emperor's portrait before having himself lashed to the compass mounting. The ship now listed so steeply that her battle-flag only just cleared the wave tops. But of more than 2,700 men aboard, only about 300 had left before the sudden end. As the last torpedo struck, the remaining shells, torn lose in *Yamato's* magazines by the list, set off a chain of internal explosions. At 1423, with a massive eruption of orange-brown smoke and flame, the last of the Japanese 'super-ships' rolled briefly upright and then slid quickly beneath the waters of the East China Sea. She had suffered at least 10 torpedoes, seven direct hits from bombs and innumerable near-misses. According to *Yahagi's* captain, with survivors in the water, the crew gave *Yamato* a last *banzai* as she disappeared. Then, while American machine-guns ripped the water all around, they began to sing the Japanese anthem.

Yamato's sacrifice was in vain; as wasted as the milliards of *yen* and years of effort Japan had squandered producing *Yamato*, and her sisters. The day of the battleship was drawing to a close before they were launched.

Richard O'Neill

The proud Yamato's *funeral pyre. This is the explosion which sent the twisted remains down into over 3,200ft of water in the East China Sea south of Kyushu on 7 April 1945. Over 2,000 of her crew and Adm. Ito went down with her.*

SANTA CRUZ 1942

With Henderson Field the key, 70 American and Japanese ships and nearly 400 aircraft clashed in unrelenting conflict

In 1942, the seemingly unstoppable expansion of Japanese imperialism threatened to engulf the whole of SE Asia and even Australia. American forces in the Pacific fought desperately to stem the tide. The Battle of the Santa Cruz Islands was of vital importance. There was no clear victor at the time but it was to significantly affect the war in the Pacific. Why?

Between May and October 1942 a series of four naval/air battles in the western Pacific established that the aircraft carrier had replaced the battleship's supremacy in the world's fleets. The battleship era was by no means completely finished and a number of vital battleship actions were still to be fought, but the aircraft-carrier had become the linch-pin of the fleet. The battleship and every other type of war-ship were now its subordinates. This change vastly increased the potential of seapower. The ability of the battleship to influence a war directly was limited to a score of miles—the range of its guns. But the carrier was a far more flexible weapon—able to strike over hundreds of miles and influence events over huge areas.

The strategic problems which the two sides faced were very similar. Guadalcanal lay at the end of a long and difficult line of communication and competed with other areas for scarce resources. The Japanese were very slow to realise the island's importance, giving more priority to the war in China and the threat of a war with Russia. The Imperial Navy therefore was forced to make do with the troops already in the SW Pacific. On the American side, Guadalcanal had to compete with the Battle of the Atlantic and the need to supply Russia. And preparations were reaching a climax for the Operation Torch landings in North Africa. It was not surprising that the Marines on Guadalcanal were soon thinking of themselves as a forgotten army.

After several months of fierce fighting neither side wanted to risk their depleted fleets without the certainty of decisive victory. The Japanese chose to wear their enemy down until they could re-establish an effective superiority. The waters between the American base at Espiritu Santo, in the New Hebrides islands, and the Solomons were so heavily patrolled by Japanese submarines that the area was dubbed 'Torpedo Junction'. Henderson Field, near Lunga Point, was in the possession of the Americans. They took advantage of this to control the waters around Guadalcanal during daylight.

A pattern of operations was soon established. American convoys delivered supplies from Espiritu Santo to their garrison while day lasted, but withdrew at night-fall. Under the cover of darkness the 'Tokyo Express' of Japanese troop-carrying destroyers and cruisers would rush down 'the Slot' to land stores and reinforcements or bombard the American positions. But they would have to leave in a hurry in order to be out of range of avenging aircraft from Henderson Field before daybreak. Thus neither side was able to achieve a superiority in ground forces on the island. The Japanese were particularly short of supplies, rather than men. They had few landing craft and had to rely on fast destroyers and small boats. The Americans found fuel for Henderson's aircraft their greatest problem.

A series of skirmishes, and minor battles established the Japanese superiority in night fighting and turned the water north of Guadalcanal into a wreck-strewn 'Ironbottom Sound'. An attempt by the Japanese to force through a larger convoy than usual resulted in another carrier battle on 24 August.

The honors of the Battle of the Eastern Solomons were fairly evenly shared. A Japanese light carrier, the *Ryujo*, was lost. The American carrier *Enterprise* was damaged and had to return to Pearl Harbor. The next weeks saw several successes for the Japanese policy of attrition. The carrier *Wasp* was sunk and the carrier *Saratoga* and the battleship *North Carolina* damaged. At one time the Americans had only one carrier in the Guadalcanal area. Better news for the Americans came with the Battle of Cape Esperance on 11 October when a Japanese cruiser force was severely damaged in a night action.

By this time the Japanese had decided to break the stale-mate on Guadalcanal, which was also delaying the progress of the New Guinea campaign. In mid-September Imperial Army and Navy Staffs agreed that: 'After reinforcement of Army forces has been completed, Army and Navy forces will combine and in one action attack and retake Guadal-

'Pugnacious and determined' characterises Vice Admiral William F. Halsey, Commander, South Pacific Area.

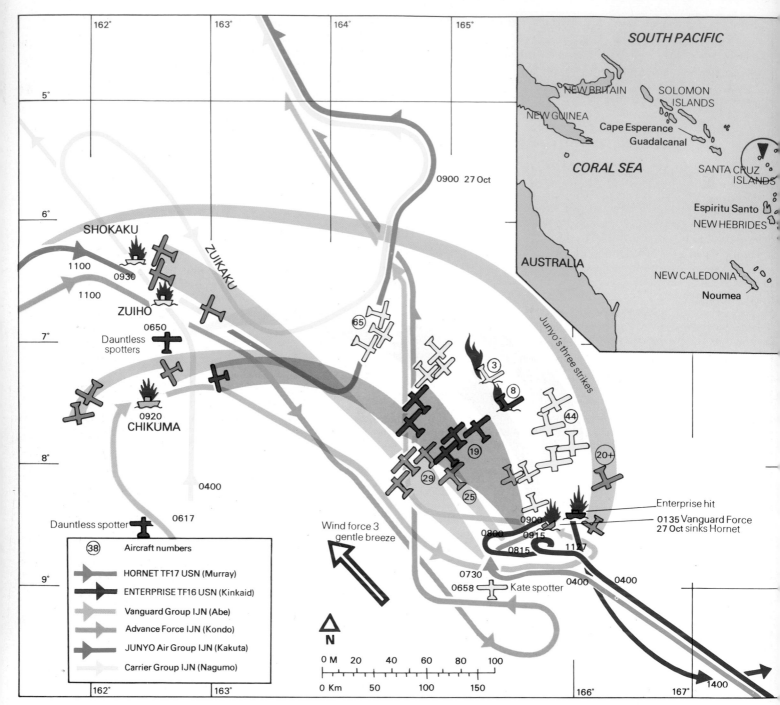

SOUTH PACIFIC

NEW BRITAIN

SOLOMON ISLANDS

NEW GUINEA

Cape Esperance
Guadalcanal

CORAL SEA

SANTA CRUZ ISLANDS

Espiritu Santo
NEW HEBRIDES

AUSTRALIA

NEW CALEDONIA

Noumea

162° 163° 164° 165°

5°

0900 27 Oct

6°

SHOKAKU

1100

0930

1100

ZUIKAKU

ZUIHO

0650

Dauntless
spotters

7°

65

3

8

44

CHIKUMA

0920

19

20+

8°

29

25

Enterprise hit

0400

0900

0135 Vanguard Force
27 Oct sinks Hornet

0617

0800

0915

Dauntless spotter

1127

0815

38 Aircraft numbers

Wind force 3
gentle breeze

0730

HORNET TF17 USN (Murray)

0658

0400

0400

ENTERPRISE TF16 USN (Kinkaid)

0900

Kate spotter

Vanguard Group IJN (Abe)

Advance Force IJN (Kondo)

JUNYO Air Group IJN (Kakuta)

Carrier Group IJN (Nagumo)

N

9°

0 M 20 40 60 80 100

0 Km 50 100 150

162° 163° 166° 167° 1400

Junyo's three strikes

Naval battles can be confusing, but at Santa Cruz air-strikes by both sides must be added in two dimensions.

canal Island airfield. During this operation the Navy will take all necessary action to halt the efforts of the enemy to augment his forces in the Solomons area.' The capture of the airfield was left to the Army. After its experience at Midway, the Navy was apparently chary of risking a major battle while the enemy had the use of an 'unsinkable aircraft carrier'—Henderson Field. During October the 'Tokyo Express' increased its work, with heavy bombardments of Henderson Field and other American positions. It brought the Japanese strength on the island up to 20,000 men.

The Americans were fully aware of their own danger. On 15 October Admiral Chester W. Nimitz, C-in-C in the Pacific, considered that his forces could not control the sea. Supplying American positions could be done, but only at great military cost. By 18 October Vice Admiral William F. Halsey had been appointed to succeed Vice Admiral Robert

L. Ghormley as Comsopac (Commander, South Pacific Area). Halsey's reputation in the Pacific was second to none. He had commanded the carrier task forces which had first struck back at the all-conquering Japanese and in particular had commanded the group from which the Doolittle Raid on Tokyo was launched. His strategy was 'Kill Japs! Kill more Japs!' At last, with the Torch convoy on its way, Washington was prepared to increase its support of the South Pacific operations.

The Japanese had planned to capture Henderson Field on 21 October, but the unexpected strength of the American garrison (which rose to over 23,000 Marines and GIs) caused them to postpone the attack until 23 October. The delay did not do them much good. They lost over 2,000 men and all their tanks. However on the 24th Admiral Isokuru Yamamoto, the Japanese naval C-in-C, warned his military

UNITED STATES SOUTH PACIFIC FORCE

Comsopac	Vice-Adm. Halsey
TASK FORCE 16	Rear-Adm. Kinkaid
Aircraft Carrier (1)	**Enterprise**; Air Group 10
83 aircraft	34 F4F-4 Grumman Wildcats
	36 SBD-3 Douglas Dauntless dive bombers
	13 TBF-1 Grumman Avenger torpedo bombers
Battleship (1)	South Dakota
Cruisers (2)	Portland San Juan (AA)
Destroyers (8)	Porter Mahan Cushing Preston Smith Maury Conyngham Shaw
TASK FORCE 17	Rear-Adm. Murray
Aircraft Carrier (1)	**Hornet**; Air Group 8
88 aircraft	36 F4F-4 36-SBD-3 16 TBF-1
Cruisers (4)	Northampton Pensacola San Diego Juneau (AA)
Destroyers (6)	Morris Anderson Hughes Mustin Russell Barton

Total ships = 23 warships **Total aircraft** = 171

JAPANESE COMBINED FLEET

C-in-C (at Truk)	Adm. Yamamoto in Yamato
ADVANCE FORCE	Vice-Adm. Kondo
Cruisers (5)	Atago Takao Myoko Mayo Isuzu
Destroyers (6)	Naganami Makinami Takanami Umikaze Kawakaze Suzukaze
Air Group	Rear-Adm. Kakuta
Aircraft Carrier (1)	**Junyo**
55 aircraft	24 Mitsubishi A6M ('Zeke') Zero fighters
	21 Aichi D3A ('Val') dive bombers
	10 Nakajima B5N ('Kate') torpedo bombers
Destroyers (2)	Kuroshio Hayashio
Support Group	Vice-Adm. Kurita
Battleships (2)	Kongo Haruna
Destroyers (6)	Samidare Yudachi Harusame Oyashio Kagero Murasame
STRIKING FORCE Carrier Group	Vice-Adm. Nagumo
Aircraft Carriers (3)	**Shokaku** 18 'Zeke' 20 'Val'
61 aircraft	23 'Kate'
72 aircraft	**Zuikaku** 27 'Zeke' 27 'Val' 18 'Kate'
24 aircraft	**Zuiho** 18 'Zeke' 6 'Kate'
Cruisers (1)	Kumano
Destroyers (8)	Amatsukaze Hatsukaze Tokitsukaze Yukikaze Arashi Maikaze Teruzuki Hamamaze
Vanguard Group	Rear-Adm. Abe
Battleships (2)	Hiei Kirishima
Cruisers (4)	Nagara Tone Chikuma Suzuya
Destroyers (7)	Kazagumo Makigumo Yugumo Akigumo Tanikaze Urakaze Isokaze

Total ships = 47 warships
Total aircraft = 212

colleagues that the fleet, which had been at sea since 11 October, was running dangerously short of fuel and would soon have to withdraw. The attacks on Henderson Field therefore continued and a false report of victory in the early hours of 25 October brought the Japanese fleet hurrying south, only to reverse their course as soon as the report was denied. At 1200, two Japanese carriers were spotted by a Catalina flying boat but they immediately turned away and so avoided the search aircraft of the American carriers.

Another night of doubt and indecision followed for both fleets. On land the Japanese mounted another attack, but were eventually forced to admit defeat. The first part of the Japanese plan had failed. The outcome of the land attack was so uncertain that the units of their fleet had been drawn much farther south than intended. On the night of 25/26 October elements of the Japanese navy were twice sighted and attacked by Catalinas. In his headquarters at Noumea, in New Caledonia, Admiral Halsey was in no doubt what his orders to his commanders at sea should be: 'Attack—Repeat—Attack!'

The exact composition of the two fleets is shown in the tables. Task Force 64, led by Rear Admiral Willis A. Lee, in *Washington*, was responsible for protecting Guadalcanal from night bombardments and operated independently throughout the battle. During the night of 25/26 October, the battleship *Washington* was patrolling west of Savo Island. Task Force 16, under Rear Admiral Thomas C. Kinkaid, was based on the carrier *Enterprise*. Rear Admiral George D. Murray commanded Task Force 17 from the carrier *Hornet*.

Veterans of the Pacific war

Enterprise and *Hornet* were sister-ships, completed in 1938 and 1941 respectively. In October 1942 they were the last word in carrier design and represented the fruits of the USN's inter-war experience of aircraft carriers. With a displacement of 19,000 tons (*Enterprise*) and 20,000 tons (*Hornet*) they were capable of speeds up to 34 knots and could operate between 80 and 100 planes. Both ships were veterans of the Pacific war, having worked together on the Doolittle Raid to Tokyo and at Midway.

The battleship *South Dakota* of Task Force 16 was one of a new generation of fast ships. With a displacement of 35,000 tons, she was capable of 28 knots and had a main armament of nine 16in guns. She was fresh from Pearl Harbor where her AA guns had been increased to include 68 of the new 40mms in quadruple mounts and 78 20mm guns. Captain Thomas L. Gatch, her commander, neglecting the conventional 'bull', had concentrated on gunnery practice. The battle that followed proved that he had made a trained and efficient fighting team of his inexperienced ship's company.

The Japanese divided their fleet into a number of smaller units as well, but on principles which differed significantly from those of the Americans. The two main elements were the Advance Force, under Vice Admiral Nobutake Kondo, in *Atago*, and the Striking Force under Vice Admiral Chuichi Nagumo. The Advance Force was intended for the close support of the troops on Guadalcanal and had been responsible for most of the night bombardments of the American positions during October. On 26 October it consisted of two battleships, four heavy cruisers and a destroyer screen. Originally two carriers had provided air cover, but *Hiyo* had developed engine trouble and had been forced to return to Truk on 22 October. This left only her sister ship *Junyo*, completed as recently as May. Both ships were converted passenger liner hulls. For their size, 24,000 tons, they carried a small complement of aircraft, just over 50, and were underpowered, being capable of only $25\frac{1}{2}$ knots.

The Striking Force to deal with any major interference by the American fleet, was sub-divided into a Carrier Group under Nagumo, of three aircraft carriers and their screen and a Vanguard Force under Rear Admiral Hiroaki Abe of two battleships, three heavy cruisers and a destroyer screen. The carriers *Shokaku* and *Zuikaku* were sister-ships, designed as fleet carriers to work with the *Yamato*-class super-battleships. They displaced 25,000 tons, but with engines capable of 160,000 SHP they had a speed of 34 knots. Able to handle air groups of over 80 planes, they had operated together at Pearl Harbor and the Coral Sea. Damage in the latter battle ensured that they missed Midway. *Zuiho* was a light carrier, originally designed as a submarine tender. Displacing 11,000 tons, she could reach 28 knots with up to 30 aircraft.

The Japanese practice of dividing their fleets into sections has been criticised. The fault lay not so much in the division itself but the way in which it was done. By separating the individual parts too much and dividing their carriers between the parts they generally ensured that only a fraction of their available carrier strength would be able to intervene in any battle. This happened at Midway and, to a lesser extent, at Santa Cruz. Within the main divisions of the fleet, the carriers operated as a unit, but without the support of other types of ship, save destroyers. Although this made it easier to co-ordinate aircraft operations, it meant that the carriers were exposed to air attack.

Once their carriers were sighted, all the Japanese eggs were in one basket. And they lacked the fearsome AA fire of the Americans. At Midway four Japanese carriers were caught together and three were sunk. The fourth escaped temporarily because of a fortuitous rainstorm. On the other hand the Japanese, although they sighted one American carrier group at Midway, remained ignorant for a long time of the presence of another, stronger, group. A further Japanese disadvantage was that their carriers had restricted bridges and limited radio facilities. This made them unsuitable as flag-ships, yet they had to be used as such.

First light on 26 October came shortly after 0500, revealing a fine day, with just enough cloud in the sky to conceal a dive-bomber attack. The American carriers were by then north of the Santa Cruz Islands. They chose to approach Guadalcanal from that direction rather than risk encountering Japanese submarine patrols in Torpedo Junction. Their course was north-westerly and less than 200 miles ahead of them were the Japanese forces in a triangular formation. The Vanguard Group of the Japanese Striking Force was leading the carriers by 60 miles. One hundred miles to the west was the Advanced Force, with the carrier *Junyo* maneuvering independently even farther west. The Japanese forces were all steering northwards. Both sides were aware that the enemy's carriers were at sea, but neither knew the other's exact location. Delays in transmission meant that Kinkaid had not received the report of the Catalina which had attacked *Zuikaku* during the night. This was unfortunate because the overwhelming advantage in carrier battles went to the side which struck first. Kinkaid ordered an aircraft search from *Enterprise*. Sixteen Dauntless dive bombers took off. Each was armed with a 500lb bomb. They fanned in pairs to the north and west. One group saw a 'Kate' torpedo bomber on a similar mission and at 0617 the Vanguard Group, led by Admiral Abe, was sighted. There was no sign of the carriers until 0650. The first pair of scouts could not break through the fighter patrols. Then at 0740 another pair, having heard the sighting report and altered course, made an unobserved approach. They attacked the light carrier *Zuiho* and both scored a hit. A 50ft hole in the flight deck made the carrier useless. But it was too late to prevent a strike taking off.

The 'Kate' spotted by *Enterprise's* aircraft had identified a carrier task force at 0658. At 0700 a 65-strong force of 'Zekes', 'Kates' and 'Vals' flew off and another group was

USNA

30

▷ *The signal bridge of the* Hornet, *left a pile of scorched and twisted steel after a suicide dive by a crippled Japanese plane. But it was not long before the true Kamikaze suicide squads took to the air to throw their lives away in cold and deliberate self-destruction, flying in aircraft that carried only enough fuel to get them to their targets.*

◁▽ *Top ship in this interesting photograph is the USS* South Dakota, *35,000-ton battleship, which had been hit on the corner of the forward triple 16in gun-turret during the battle of Santa Cruz. Splinters from the bomb wounded the ship's commander, Capt. Gatch, as he stood on the bridge. No. 2 turret is depressed as the guns are overhauled before the Guadalcanal battle to come. The 680ft long battleship is lying alongside USS* Prometheus, *special repair-ship at anchor off Noumea.*

▽ *A 'Kate' torpedo-bomber passes an American cruiser at Santa Cruz.*

Imperial War Museum

USNA

31

soon being ranged. The American carriers did nothing about their sighting reports until 0720. Even then, the attack was not co-ordinated. At 0730 15 Dauntless, six Avenger torpedo bombers and eight Wildcat fighters left *Hornet*. *Enterprise's* first strike consisted of eight Avengers and eight Wildcats and only three Dauntlesses. The carrier was by now critically short of dive bombers. Six had not returned from the previous evening's attempt to find the Japanese carriers, six more were on anti-submarine patrol, and the 16 scouts had not yet come back. The *Enterprise's* strike flew off at 0800 and was followed at 0815 by *Hornet's* second strike—nine Dauntlesses, nine Avengers and seven Wildcats. With their targets nearly 200 miles away there was neither time nor fuel for the aircraft to circle the carriers until a concentrated strike could be built up. Squadrons flew in a long-drawn-out gaggle. As they flew they passed the incoming Japanese strike. Some Japanese fighters left their convoy to attack the *Enterprise* group. Four Wildcat and four Avengers were either shot down or severely damaged and forced back to the carrier. The size of the *Enterprise's* strike had been halved at a cost of only three 'Zekes'.

The American fleet was expecting the Japanese strike. Every possible step was taken to avoid a disastrous carrier fire, such as that which had destroyed the *Lexington* at the Coral Sea. Aircraft were secured in the hangar deck, aviation fuel lines were filled with carbon dioxide and damage control parties were on constant alert. Speed was maintained at 28 knots and around the carriers their escorts were poised to provide massive AA fire.

The first line of defense was the 38 Wildcats of the combat air patrol (CAP). This was directed from the *Enterprise*. But the officer in charge was new to his job, having recently replaced a Midway veteran whom Halsey had taken to Noumea. For some time the fighter-direction team could not distinguish between the American and Japanese air groups on their cluttered radar screens. It was 0857 before a clear picture emerged. The CAP was too near the fleet, and too late—only 10 miles out at 0906. Although the Wildcats claimed some victims, neither they nor the American gunners could break the co-ordination of the Japanese attack.

At about 0900 *Enterprise's* group was hidden by a rain squall. This left *Hornet*—lacking the close support of a battleship like *South Dakota*—to face the full might of the Japanese attack alone. 'Val' dive bombers began the assault, scoring one hit and two near-misses. The squadron commander, his plane having been hit, made no attempt to drop his bombs but kept on diving. The 'Val' bounced off the carrier's funnel and burnt through the flight-deck. The dive-bombers suffered heavily, but their attack covered the approach of a squadron of 'Kate' torpedo bombers from astern. Two torpedoes crashed into *Hornet's* engine-rooms and she slowed to a halt under a pall of black smoke. A sitting target, *Hornet* was hit by three more bombs and then a burning 'Kate' made a suicide run into the ship's port side. It was all over in 10 minutes. The Japanese had lost 25 planes, but the once-formidable *Hornet* was a listing, blazing wreck.

Meanwhile the American air groups were approaching the Japanese fleet. But their straggling formation had been disturbed by the fighters. They were unable to deliver a united attack, or even find the same target. Fifteen Dauntlesses from *Hornet* led the attack. The first wave of defending fighters was kept at bay by their escorting Wildcats but the Dauntlesses were then left without protection. At 0930

Shokaku and *Zuiho* appeared below and the main Japanese CAP above. Even so, 11 bombers got through and scored between three and six hits on *Shokaku*. The 1,000lb bombs tore her flight-deck apart and started a tremendous blaze in the hangar. But there were no torpedo bombers to finish the job. *Hornet's* Avengers had lost touch with the rest of the strike and so *Shokaku* and *Zuiho* went unmolested as they limped towards Truk. The Avengers made contact with Abe's Vanguard Group, but they were so short of fuel that they could not continue to search for the carriers. At 0930 they made an unsuccessful attack on the cruiser *Suzuya*. The rest of the American aircraft also missed the carriers and attacked Abe's group. *Hornet's* second wave damaged the cruiser *Chikuma* but *Enterprise's* aircraft had no luck at all.

As the American aircraft turned for home the result of the battle was still very much in the balance. Two Japanese carriers were out of action, but the second strike from *Shokaku* and *Zuikaku* had not yet attacked. *Zuikaku* was ready to gather up the survivors of all three carriers and prepare another strike. *Junyo* was hurrying westwards and, as Nagumo's flagship *Shokaku* was out of action, he transferred command of flying operations to Rear Admiral Kakuji Kakuta on board *Junyo*. She was still more than 300 miles from the American task forces. Even so, Kakuta ordered a strike to commence. Her aircraft were to land on *Zuikaku* or *Shokaku* after the attack.

On the American side, *Hornet's* fires had been brought under control, although at one stage the order to abandon ship had been given. By 1005 the 9,050-ton cruiser *Northampton* was ready to begin towing the carrier when an unsuccessful attack by a stray 'Val' disrupted operations.

Although Task Force 16 had not yet been attacked, it was the scene of increasing confusion. Overhead were stacked the surviving aircraft from both carriers. They were by now nearing the end of their fuel. At 1002 the destroyer *Porter* was torpedoed by a Japanese submarine while picking up the crew of a crashed aircraft. The *Porter* was so badly damaged that she had to be sunk by gunfire, her crew transferring to another destroyer, *Shaw*. A submarine was the last thing which any carrier wanted to encounter while forced to keep a straight course for aircraft to land.

Then (almost as soon as the landings started) the second Japanese strike was detected on the *South Dakota's* radar. *Enterprise* suspended operations and prepared to defend herself. Fortunately this attack was not so well co-ordinated as that on *Hornet*. The dive-bombers arrived 20 minutes before the torpedo-bombers and were met by the heaviest AA fire yet seen in the Pacific War. *South Dakota*, only 1,000 yards from *Enterprise*, showed to perfection her crew's gunnery skills. She shot down 26 'Vals', *Enterprise* claimed another seven. But two bombs found their mark, damaging the flight deck and starting fresh fires in the hangar. But the torpedo-bombers were too far behind to deliver the final blow.

When they finally arrived they were attacked by the combat air patrol. One Wildcat pilot, Lieutenant Vejtasa, shot down six before he ran out of ammunition. About 14 'Kates' got through to the Task Force. Five of these were destroyed by AA fire. Then the surviving Japanese moved in on the luckless *Enterprise*, attacking on both sides. Full-speed maneuvering by her captain once more saved the carrier. One 'Kate' did not even try to launch its torpedo, but dived straight onto the forecastle of the destroyer *Smith*. The blazing ship used *South Dakota's* wake to douse her fires and so survived the battle.

GRUMMAN 'WILDCAT' F4F-4

△ Grumman 'Wildcat' F4F-4
Engine One Pratt and Whitney R1830 radial
   giving 1,200hp
Armament Six .5in Browning MGs; 2 100lb bombs
Span 38ft
Length 28ft 9in
Height 9ft 2½in
Range 770 miles (1,239k)
Speed 318mph (512kh)

▽ Mitsubishi A6M2 Zero
Engine One Nakajima NK1C Sakae 12, 14-cylinder
   radial
Armament Two 20mm cannon; 2 7.7mm MGs
Span 39ft 4½in
Length 29ft 8¾in
Height 10ft
Range 1,930 miles (3,106k) with drop-tank
Speed 332mph (534kh)

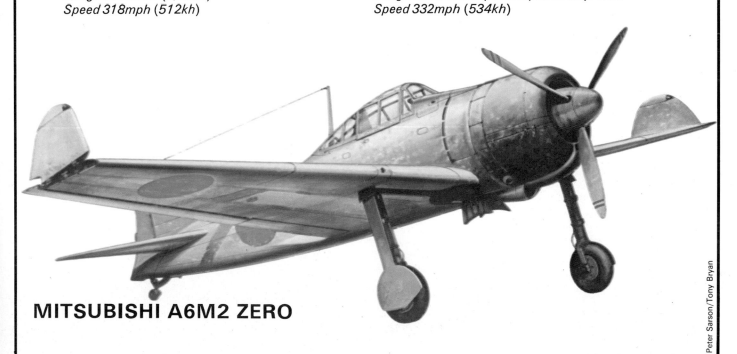

MITSUBISHI A6M2 ZERO

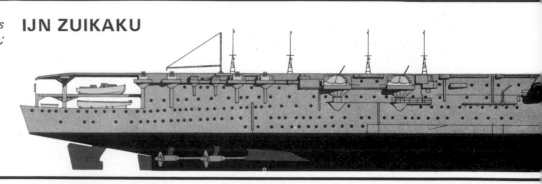

IJN ZUIKAKU

Displacement *25,675 tons*
Armor *8½in (216mm) main;*
    6¾in (171mm) deck
Armament *16 x 5in*
    36 x 25mm
Aircraft *72 operational*
Complement *1660*
Machinery *8 Kanpon*
    boilers; turbines
    gave 160,000 SHP

△ *An American cruiser successfully evades a Japanese suicide dive—the aircraft hurtles into the sea*
▽ *The air filled with AA bursts as the doomed USS Hornet comes under attack at Santa Cruz.*

On board *Enterprise*, the ship's company worked with disciplined but feverish haste to clear the flight deck and complete the recovery of the circling aircraft before they ran out of fuel. The appearance of a submarine periscope made things more difficult. Then at 1101 *Junyo's* aircraft appeared on *South Dakota's* radar screen. Alerted by this, her gunners opened fire on six unidentified aircraft at 1110. These proved to be returning Dauntlesses. By the time that this mistake had been sorted out *Junyo's* aircraft were hidden in the cloud over the Task Force. Twenty attacked in a two-minute flurry, but achieved only one near-miss on *Enterprise* and lost eight planes. At 1127 two isolated 'Vals' dived on *South Dakota* and the AA cruiser *San Juan*. One bomb exploded on *South Dakota's* foremost turret, without penetrating the armor. But Captain Gatch was wounded by splinters and for a moment the battleship was not under command.

Tight formation shattered

As *South Dakota* headed towards *Enterprise*, *San Juan* was hit astern and her rudder jammed. The tight formation of Task Force 16 was shattered as the ships maneuvered out of the way of their careering consorts. Both ships were soon under control and *Enterprise* was able to land aircraft again. But with her forward elevator out of action the carrier was slow in getting aircraft below and several planes were forced to ditch before their turn came. *Enterprise* launched a CAP, but did not attempt to renew the battle. All morning the carrier had been steering south-eastwards into the wind, but at 1400 she turned east. Admiral Kinkaid had decided that with only *Enterprise's* limited capacity to operate aircraft he could not risk an offensive against an unknown number of Japanese carriers.

USS HORNET

Displacement *20,000 tons*
Armor *4in (102mm) main;*
    3in (77mm) deck
Armament *8x5in AA;*
    16x1.1in AA;
    16x5in MGs
Aircraft *Approx 100*
Complement *2,200*
Machinery *turbines,*
    four-shaft geared,
    giving 120,000 SHP
Speed *34 knots*
Length *809½ft (245m)*
Beam *100ft (30m)*
Draught *26ft (7.9m)*

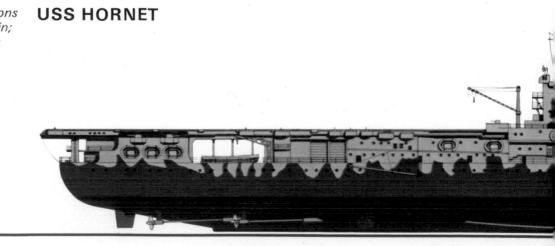

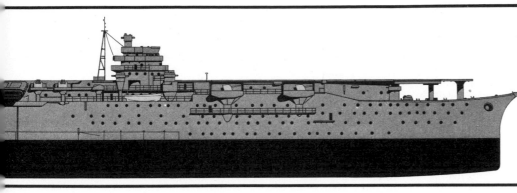

Speed 34.2 knots
Length 845ft (257.5m)
Beam 85ft 6in (26m)
Draught 29ft (8.8m)
Laid down Kawasaki,
    Kobe, 25 May, 1938
Launched 27 November 1939
Sunk 25 October 1944
Sister-ship, Shokaku,
    sunk 19 June 1944

Peter Sarson/Tony Bryan

The Japanese still had two carriers left in the battle, but had lost over 100 aircraft. *Zuikaku* and *Junyo* collected the mixed assortment of aircraft and sent them off in penny packets. Kondo and Abe also increased the speed of their battleship squadrons, hoping to finish off the crippled American ships after nightfall.

The cruiser *Northampton* was inching *Hornet* to safety when they were spotted at 1515 by Japanese aircraft. *Northampton* cut her tow, leaving the stationary carrier an easy target for the approaching torpedo planes. One hit was enough to seal her fate. The order to abandon ship was given, but three more Japanese formations attacked before all the survivors had been taken off. Then *Hornet* showed the same endurance as her sister-ship *Yorktown* at Midway. Destroyers fired nine torpedoes into her and over 400 5in shells. But *Hornet*, burning from stern to stern, was still afloat when she was sighted by Abe's ships at 2120. The Japanese at least had the satisfaction of avenging the Doolittle Raid by giving the *coup de grâce* to the ship which launched it.

During the night, the Japanese carriers were once again attacked by Catalinas. It was not until the afternoon of the 27th that the Combined Fleet began its withdrawal to Truk.

At the end of the battle neither side had suffered decisive losses. The Americans had lost *Hornet* and a destroyer. *Enterprise*, *South Dakota*, *San Juan* and a destroyer had been damaged. No major Japanese unit had been sunk, but two carriers and a destroyer had been damaged. *Shokaku* was out of action for nine months. The Japanese also lost 100 aircraft, against American casualties of 20 planes destroyed in action and another 54 missing or damaged.

What was the final result of the battle? Admiral Samuel E. Morison claims in the Official History of the battle, 'The Struggle for Guadalcanal', that 'Measured in combat tonnage sunk, the Japanese had won a tactical victory; but other losses forced them back to the Truk hideout'. This is less than fair to the Japanese. Truk was no more a 'hideout' than Noumea and the American fleet turned for home first. The real reason for the retirement of the Japanese fleet was the failure of their army to capture Henderson Field. The struggle for Guadalcanal reverted to its former pattern: supply runs by day and night and a long, hard fight on land. Eventually the Americans won the reinforcement battle and in February 1943 Japan evacuated the survivors of her garrison.

With the advantage of hindsight it would be easy to argue that the Battle of Santa Cruz made little difference to the final result. But this is to ignore the question of what might have been. After Santa Cruz the Japanese had four undamaged carriers and the Americans had only the damaged *Enterprise* and the escort carrier *Long Island* in the Pacific. Japan had the opportunity to exploit her carrier superiority and win the decisive victory which had escaped both sides. She failed to do so because, although she had the carriers, both aircraft and pilots were lacking.

The Japanese fleet, lacking both air cover and the striking power of the carrier, could not check the American daylight convoys. By the time the Japanese carrier fleet had been repaired and re-equipped it was too late to save Guadalcanal. When the two fleets next met, in the Philippine Sea in June 1944, Japan could send only nine carriers and 430 aircraft against 15 carriers and 891 aircraft. Whether or not Santa Cruz was a setback for the Americans it bought them enough time to ensure final victory.

Michael Orr

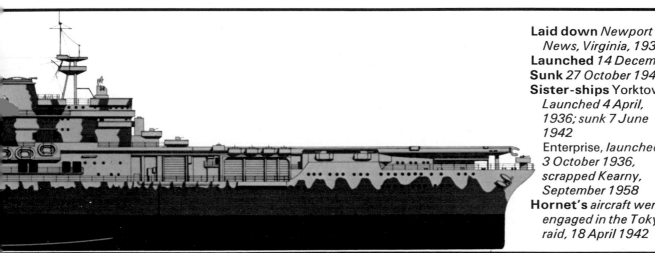

Laid down Newport
    News, Virginia, 1938
Launched 14 December 1940
Sunk 27 October 1942
Sister-ships Yorktown,
    *Launched 4 April,
    1936; sunk 7 June
    1942*
    Enterprise, *launched
    3 October 1936,
    scrapped Kearny,
    September 1958*
Hornet's *aircraft were
    engaged in the Tokyo
    raid, 18 April 1942*

Peter Sarson/Tony Bryan

TARAWA

Waist deep in water under a withering fire, the Marines struggled ashore. Could so tiny an island be worth this toll?

The shattered face of Betio a month after the assault. The long pier was a key point in the battle; from it, a withering fire exacted a heavy toll on Marines as they

approached the beaches on either side. The airstrip, clearly seen here, was an asset to the US forces in later raids on Japanese strongholds in the Marshalls.

Betio Island, on the central Pacific atoll of Tarawa, is an insignificant coral hump topped with coconut palms. It is two miles long, less than half a mile wide, and nowhere more than 9ft above sea level. Between the two world wars most people in Britain, which owned the place, had never heard of it. Today, you need a large-scale map to find it. But in 1943, Betio was a key link in the chain of island fortresses which guarded the perimeter of Japan's Pacific conquests — a chain which the Allies had to break, however bloodily.

Since their shattering sneak attack on Pearl Harbor on 7 December 1941 had seriously weakened the US Pacific Fleet, the Japanese had seized the Philippines, Wake, Guam, the Gilberts, Malaya, Burma and the Netherlands East Indies, and installed themselves in the Bismarck Archi-pelago-New Guinea-Solomons area. They were poised for their final onslaughts in New Guinea, and to attack Fiji, Samoa and New Caledonia.

Their strategy was simple: take all the island bases, isolate Australia — by cutting the US-Australia supply lines — and leave the Allies with no base in the south Pacific from which to mount a counter-offensive.

But by the end of 1942, with an enormous perimeter of bases to supply and defend, the Japanese had over-reached themselves. Frustrated in their repeated attempts to take Port Moresby in New Guinea, and seriously weakened by the Allied victories in the Coral Sea and Bismarck Sea, with their fleet crippled by the costly failure of Midway, they were no longer capable of offensive action. The tide had turned.

In planning their counter-offensive, the Allies had two choices — to start from Australia and work northwards, 'rolling up' the occupying Japanese forces as they went, or to drive a wedge into the middle of the Japanese defensive arc. At a meeting in Casablanca, French Morocco, attended by President Roosevelt and Prime Minister Churchill and their chiefs of staff, the first plan was rejected as too slow and costly. Instead they chose the 'wedge' attack, which would isolate Japan from her enormous perimeter of bases and permit an attack directly against the Japanese mainland.

A drive through the Marshalls and Carolines, via the Gilberts and Nauru Island, was the obvious first step. On 20 July 1943, the US Joint Chiefs of Staff sent a signal to Fleet Admiral Chester W. Nimitz, Pacific Fleet, instructing him to 'organize and train the necessary forces to capture, occupy, defend and develop basis in the Gilbert group....'

Tarawa atoll, in the Gilberts, was Nimitz's prime target.

Eighty miles north of the equator, it was the most strongly fortified base in the group, with an airfield constructed on its main island, Betio. Like other islands in the Japanese outer perimeter, it had a strengthened garrison and a tough, experienced commander. His instructions were to destroy the enemy at the shoreline. Should the enemy succeed in landing, his forces were to counter-attack to delay the invaders for as long as possible and exact the greatest possible punishment.

The Betio garrison numbered 4,836 men, including highly trained members of the 3rd Special Base Force and the

across — represented the most complete defensive system Japanese ingenuity could devise. It certainly was the most heavily defended atoll that would ever be invaded by Allied forces in the Pacific — a bastion which, Shibasaki boasted to his men, could not be taken by the Americans 'with a million men in a hundred years'.

Nimitz's main problem was one of logistics. In the south-west Pacific, General Douglas MacArthur had perfected island hopping and assault techniques which had neces-sitated the construction of massive bases where troops could be trained and, when wanted, could be conveyed into

Robert Hunt Library/U.S. Marine Corps

Their .5 machine-guns at the ready, Marines of the second assault wave go in, their amtracs making heavy going in the strong wind outside the lagoon entrance. In the

background can be seen troops of the third wave of attackers. The lessons learned here led to the production of greatly-improved landing craft for future assaults.

Sasebo 7th Special Naval Landing Force commanded by Rear Admiral Keiji Shibasaki.

And the island they defended — 291 acres, shaped like an old-fashioned musket and surrounded by a coral reef that barely submerges at low tide — had been organized for all-round defense on the beaches.

A network of obstacles

Along the western and south western coasts were 7.7mm light machine-guns, sited in open emplacements to provide anti-aircraft fire. On the northern coast there were more 7.7s, and 13mm heavy machine-guns as well, positioned to give flanking fire along the front of the artificial barriers (in the shape of concrete tetrahedrons) placed all along the reef. The basic weapons were complemented by a network of obstacles including anti-tank ditches, beach barricades, log fences and concrete barriers, and double-apron barbed-wire fences in the water near the beach.

And backing them up were 18 naval guns, 27 field guns, six howitzers and seven tanks mounting 37mm guns. The weapons were mounted in strongly constructed emplace-ments of coconut logs, reinforced concrete and revetted sand.

In fact, what awaited the American Marines on this tiny island — only two miles long and fewer than 800 yards

action by beaching craft. Because of the short distances involved in island-hopping, the actual movements of troops had become what amounted to colossal ferryboat opera-tions.

Gigantic mobile base

But for the Gilberts invasion, codenamed Operation Galvanic, there were no large land masses from which air support could be provided, no readily-available pools of labor, no dockyards, factories, airfields. Something new was needed — a gigantic mobile base which could provide the supply requirements for ships operating thousands of miles from US territory.

Next to Nimitz in the chain of command was Vice Admiral Raymond A. Spruance, Commander, Central Pacific Forces, under whom was the 5th Amphibious Force. For training and controlling troop elements for future amphibious landings in the Central Pacific, a separate command was created — the 5th Amphibious Corps, com-manded by Major General Holland M. Smith, USMC. For the Gilberts invasion, Gen. Smith had at his disposal the 2nd Marine Division, commanded by Major General Julian C. Smith, USMC, and the 27th Infantry Division, com-manded by Major General Ralph C. Smith.

Gen. Holland Smith's plan called for the landing of three battalion landing teams abreast on Red Beaches One, Two and Three on the north (lagoon) shore of Betio. The first three assault waves would be made up of amtracs, the fourth wave would be tanks boated in LCMs, the fifth would be LCVPs, each carrying about 35 troops.

The first troops to land would be, from east to west, the 2nd Battalion, 8th Marines; 2nd Battalion, 2nd Marines; and 3rd Battalion, 2nd Marines. The 1st Battalion, 2nd Marines, was to be held in regimental reserve. In division

◁ *Bristling with heavy machine-guns, LVT(2)s plough on. On the horizon, a* Fletcher-*class destroyer shells Betio to 'soften up' the defence ready for the landing. Delays in getting the landing craft ashore gave the Japanese time to recover from the preliminary bombardment and greet the Marines with a fierce fire; for later assault landings, bombardments were timed to the minute and were not lifted until the troops were within yards of the shore.*
◁ ▽ *With fixed bayonets, a platoon of Marines crouches behind the inadequate shelter of the seawall on beach Red Three, waiting for the signal to resume the attack.*
▽ *Two Marines dash forward with satchels of TNT to deal with a Japanese bunker. Others are already in position, ready to blast their way in. The backdrop of palm trees shredded by gunfire is evidence of the battle's ferocity.*

reserve, to be committed when and where the situation warranted, were the 1st and 3rd Battalions of the 8th Marines.

One problem, however, Admiral Nimitz could not solve: the probable depth of water above the fringing reef off the north coast of the island. The 2nd Marine Division was able to muster only 125 amphibious tractors. These LVTs (or 'amtracs') could operate through water and over land, and to them the reefs offered no great obstacle. But the remainder of the invasion force would have to be carried in standard LCVPs and when fully loaded, these drew at least 3ft 6in. Thus a minimum of 4ft of water was essential if the landing craft were to carry the assault troops from ship to shore. If not, the Marines would have to wade for several hundred yards under a hail of close-range fire.

On 13 November ships of the Northern Attack Force (Task Force 53) under Admiral R. K. Turner, which had come from Hawaii, rendezvoused with those of the Southern Attack Force (Task Force 52) under Rear Admiral Harry W. Hill, which had been based in New Zealand waters. The two forces set parallel courses for the Gilberts, Task Force 53 for Makin (a lightly-defended island) and Task Force 52 for Tarawa.

As the invasion force approached Tarawa in the early hours of 20 November, the weather was fair. The wind was E.S.E. at 13 knots. There would be relatively little surf on the beaches or inside the lagoon.

Adm. Hill, aboard his flagship *Maryland,* signalled the transports to approach the lagoon entrance, some six miles from the selected beaches. At 0335 the signal sounded for the landing craft to be launched. Ten transports carrying the amtracs lowered the landing craft into the water. Drivers took them to the sides of three other transports which had been prepared with heavy scrambling nets hanging down their sides for the Marines to clamber down into the amtracs.

Meanwhile, LCVPs boats had been disgorged from the LSTs, and the men of the second and third assault waves were loaded into them. Soon there were craft dotting the area, bobbing and circling. At a signal to the drivers, the scattered craft, full of silent troops, began to move to the assault wave assembly area northwest of the lagoon.

Not far away in the darkness lay the island. It could clearly be seen, small, flat and unimposing. Many of the unblooded enlisted men and junior officers felt optimism and relief at the sight of it. The low-lying strip of land certainly looked a pushover. 'Don't let it fool you,' murmured a Guadalcanal veteran, who knew the Japanese would fight to the death.

A star-shell suddenly burst over Betio. A few seconds later the flat *crack* of a gun came from the southern shore. It was a signal from Adm. Shibasaki, alerting his troops to the presence of the invasion force.

Shells began to fall

Three battleships, six cruisers and nine destroyers, the fire-support ships, were positioned in the open sea to the west of the island. Presently, the destroyer *Meade* curved sharply on the shore side of Adm. Hill's flagship *Maryland* and began to lay a smoke-screen. A few seconds later the battleship catapult-launched her Kingfisher spotting plane. Suddenly the Japanese batteries opened fire and shells began to fall among the ships. The splashes from near-misses were prodigious, proving that the enemy's coastal defense guns had not been knocked out by pre-invasion bombing of the past few days.

The first salvo fired by the Americans came from the battleship *Colorado* at 0507 to be followed at once by shells from the other support vessels. *Maryland's* 16in guns opened up on the southwestern point of Betio, her target the Japanese 8in coastal guns. The defenders countered with fire from all along the island. At 0542 the ships ceased firing, uncertain what damage they had caused in the pall of smoke and dust now lying over the island.

This was the moment for the carrier-based aircraft to take over — but they were nowhere in sight. Transports *Zeitin* and *Haywood,* still unloading troops into landing craft, were caught without covering fire, and shells from the shore-batteries began to splash around them. Adm. Hill immediately ordered them back out of range. Then he ordered the resumption of the naval bombardment, then cut it again as the planes appeared.

It was still dark as the Navy Hellcats swarmed in low across the sea for their first strafing attack. As soon as they had gone, dive-bombers peeled off and attacked the gun positions. Then, high up, came formations of Liberators which pattern-bombed the island from end to end. The attack lasted seven minutes, then the planes were gone.

A brief pause, then the pre-landing naval bombardment resumed. For two and a half hours the Marines in the approaching landing craft watched as the US warships threw more than 3,000 tons of projectiles at the tiny island,

pounding gun emplacements and installations, setting fire to log barricades, splintering palm trees, blasting craters and throwing up great piles of sand and coral. Across the island hung a haze of smoke and dust, broken by pillars of fire where ammunition and fuel supplies had been hit.

The first three, rather ragged waves of amtracs, carrying nearly 2,000 Marines, were on their way, heading for the lagoon entrance. Many of the Marines watched the bombardment with relief, believing that nothing could survive such a battering, that the Japanese defenders would be smashed by the time they reached the beaches.

In the first wave, there were 42 LVT(1)s, with eight empty tractors following as emergency support; 24 LVT(2)s in the second wave, and 21 in the third, followed by five replacements. The smaller warships came in with them. Minesweepers *Pursuit* and *Requisite,* screened by smoke, slipped into the lagoon and began marking the line of departure, boat lanes and dangerous shoals. Destroyers *Ringgold* and *Dashiell* came in behind them and took up positions from where they could cover the landing waves. They stood off and hammered at the Japanese shore batteries with their forward 5in guns.

Ringgold took two hits. Both were 'duds', but they still knocked out her port engine. A minute later a lucky shell found a Japanese ammunition dump and it went up in an enormous explosion, leaving the island in a grey-black shroud, broken by splashes of flame. *Pursuit* was now hove-to at the line of departure with her searchlight turned on the passage through the reef, guiding the assault waves.

But things were going wrong. A strong westerly wind and a heavy sea swell running with it was slowing down the landing craft, throwing the operation behind. Adm. Hill's spotter planes confirmed this from above, and he was forced to postpone H-hour — the actual landing — from 0830 to 0845, then to 0900.

Strafing mission was too early

His messages, however, failed to reach the fighter planes whose job it was to strafe the beaches just before the troops landed. They came in on their strafing mission far too early — at 0825 — and the naval gunfire had to be lifted until they were clear of the target. One landing craft, an LCVP, landed on the edge of the reef. From it scrambled Lieutenant William Hawkins, leading in half of his 2nd Scout-Sniper Platoon, whose orders were to fight their way to the defended pier on the north side of the island and provide a diversion while the first waves of assault troops stormed the beach heads.

But for most of the landing craft, the delayed H-hour was still too early by at least 15 minutes. Adm. Hill ordered the bombardment to cease by 0855, except for that from the two destroyers, feeling that it would endanger the assault troops as they moved towards the shore. Instead he ordered another air-strike. But the interval gave the Japanese time to recover from the naval bombardment, reinforce their beach positions, and direct accurate fire on the approaching assault force.

Now the first waves of amtracs were coming in, heading for the three beaches: Red One, which stretched 700 yards from the northwest tip of the island and halfway to the pier; Red Two, which covered the rest of the distance to the pier; and Red Three, which stretched 800 yards from the pier to a point opposite the end of the airstrip.

The long wooden pier dominated the landing area, and as the amtracs came into range they were met with blistering

The South Pacific, showing the Gilberts' vital position.

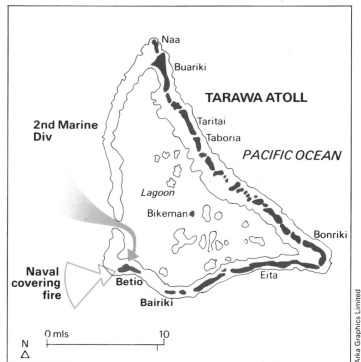

Betio. US objective on Tarawa atoll's coral reef.

fire, causing many casualties. Drivers found the lagoon so cluttered with coral blocks that amtracs trying to reach the western side had to turn and come in on the east. Some of the amtracs had hit the apron of the reef and were crawling along it. Landing Team One was steering for Red One, where the reef apron was wide and the beachline formed a sharp re-entry angle into the lagoon.

The Japanese were waiting for them. At 100 yards range they opened up with coast defense guns, light and heavy machine-guns, and rifles. Bullets rattled into the tractors' sides and shells hit the water among the wallowing craft. The Marines returned the fire with rifles and machine-guns, but their shooting from bobbing 'platforms' had little effect. There was still 70 yards to go. The Japanese fire became intense, killing most of the amtrac drivers and knocking out many of the vehicles. A tractor took a hit and burst into flames. Men became human torches and jumped into the water. As one driver was hit and slumped over, a lieutenant took over and drove the vehicle. A few seconds later he also

was hit. Then a shell struck the boat. The Marines sprawled out into 2ft of water and were caught in withering fire from a pillbox.

Hawkins' men of the 2nd Scout-Sniper Platoon had fought their way to the pier. Six of them moved onto it with grenades, machine-guns and flame-throwers. They attacked any structure that might house an enemy. Two shacks hit by flame-throwers burst into flames. The pier itself caught fire. All the Japanese on the pier died.

Less than a quarter of Team One reached the beach. Under murderous fire they struggled to the cover of the sea wall and threw themselves down behind it, exhausted. Red Three's assault waves got ashore with comparative ease, but Red Two, in the center, came under concentrated fire from pillboxes and emplacements. Enfilading fire also came from strong-points on the left.

Lieutenant Colonel Herbert Amey, commander of Team Two, had his amtrac jammed in a tangle of barbed wire, and he and his men jumped into the water. A hail of machine-gun

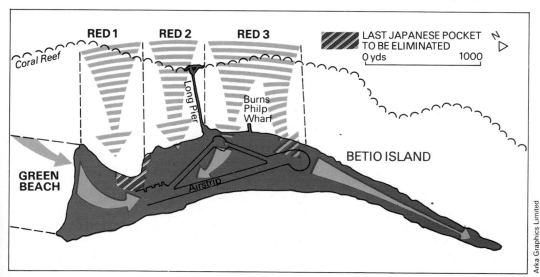

Map of Betio, showing the position of the coral reef which proved such a deadly obstacle to the Marines' attack. The landings on Red Beach on 20 November were followed by support attacks across Green Beach in the next two days. The final clearance of the 'tip of the barrel' was made on 23 November, but the last pocket of enemy resistance was close to beach Red One, scene of the initial landing.

Dead Japanese sprawled outside their heavily reinforced dugout. These bunkers — there were hundreds — were of coconut logs packed with sand and coral to cushion the blast of shellfire. Proof against machine-guns and light artillery, they finally yielded to TNT and flame-throwers.

Malcolm McGregor

A US Marine in fighting order, his clothing designed to let him fight unhampered. Those landed on Tarawa carried a weapon, most often an M1 .30 carbine, plus a minimum of personal gear — three units of K-rations, two water canteens, shaving kit, toothbrush and spoon.

fire caught them and Amey was killed with three of his men. The remainder managed to get to the shelter of a stranded boat.

Behind the first assault waves, the fourth wave, largely of 37mm guns and their crews in LCVs, reached the edge of the reef and stayed there, trapped by the tide. All they could do was sit it out until nightfall.

The fifth wave, LCMs, had to discharge their Sherman tanks in 3ft of water. Eleven tanks reached the beach after a hazardous journey over the reef. The rest were stopped by enemy fire. The tank battalion commander, Lieutenant Colonel Alexander Swenceski, was hit as he jumped into the water. Critically wounded, he managed to drag himself onto a heap of bodies before he fell unconscious.

By now the beach was an inferno. All along the shore and for some yards inland there was close, bitter and bloody fighting. Rifle fire and grenades had no effect against the well-entrenched enemy. The Marines used flame-throwers, and blocks of TNT in place of grenades, to overpower the enemy, bunker by bunker. All Lt. Hawkins' 34 snipers had

got safely ashore. They worked their way along the island shooting Japanese out of trees and blowing them out of foxholes. At one stage Hawkins was seen riding in an amtrac, bullets singing about his head, cleaning up machine-gun nests.

The commander of the initial assault, Colonel David Shoup, stood waist deep in the water, directing the battle with the aid of a radio transmitter strapped to a sergeant's back. He called for fire-support on the 'barrel' end of the island, but invaders and defenders were too close together for naval fire and carrier Hellcats were brought in to bomb and strafe the enemy positions. By 1000 hours, 23 amtracs and two LCMs full of dead and wounded were still stuck on the reef, and Japanese artillery fire was still pounding the beach-heads from emplacements on the eastern end of the island.

All through the morning of the first day the beach-head battle raged. Both sides had many heroes. One was Staff Sergeant William Bordelon, a Texan assault engineer, who had his amtrac knocked out under him. Bordelon led the four survivors ashore and began attacking enemy pillboxes — by creeping up beside them and laying demolition charges. They destroyed two, then, while attacking a third, the Texan was hit. He pressed on, using his rifle to cover other Marines scaling a wall. He made up another charge and attacked another emplacement, which he destroyed as the Japanese cut him down.

Col. Shoup had got safely ashore on Red Two beach. He quickly set up his command post on the seaward side of a Japanese bombproof shelter which was still occupied by the Japanese. The Marines could not get at the defenders

for fear of blowing up their own commander, so sentries were posted at the entrances to contain them.

By noon, the tide had still refused to rise. The waiting landing craft could not float over the coral. Many of the amtracs were corpse-strewn wrecks stuck fast on the coral. Fifteen hundred Marines were trapped on the narrow beach under the shelter of the wall.

The east flank of beach Red One was under punishing enfilading fire, which had stopped all further landings in that section. Landing Team Two held a 200-yard strip on the eastern end of the beach, but were trapped there, unable to break out. Help was needed, and quickly. Shoup, not trusting the uncertain radios, sent Lieutenant Colonel Carlson back to the *Maryland* with a terse summary.

But Gen. Julian Smith, commanding the landing force, had already assessed it and committed one battalion of reinforcements. He was left with only one infantry battalion in reserve, and it was standing by. Smith immediately ordered it to move to the line of departure. Then he signalled to Maj. Gen. Holland Smith, in command of the Gilberts joint operation, asking that the 6th Combat Team also be placed under his control. Finally, he set about organizing the remaining divisional support troops — communicators, clerks, engineers and artillery men — into infantry battalions to be thrown into the battle if necessary.

By now the LSD *Ashland* had nosed into the lagoon and some of her tanks had got ashore. They rolled up through a gap in the retaining wall and forced a way through to the interior of the island. The reserves organized by Gen. Smith poured into the lagoon, which was still covered by a lagging tide. LVTs and LCVPs floundered off the edge of the reef, jamming the approaches to the pier. Many of the landing craft had had their radios shot away and were stuck in the lagoon waiting for orders.

The amtrac battalion's commanding officer, Major Henry Drewes, had been killed and his LVTs were leaderless. By

This Japanese naval infantryman (he can be identified by the anchor on his cap and helmet) is typical of the troops that defended Tarawa. Most detachments refused to surrender while a man was still standing, and almost the only prisoners the Marines took were Korean laborers.

mid-afternoon over 100 landing craft were milling around in the lagoon waiting for orders. Of the 5,000 men who reached the shore more than 1,500 were casualties. Several hundred had been evacuated from the beach by Navy medical corpsmen, who worked all through the day under fire. The wounded were ferried out over the reef in rubber rafts for transfer to landing craft, which then took them out to the transports.

Night came as some relief to both attackers and attacked. But even after dark the divisional artillery, landing on beach Red Two, could not roll their 75mm howitzers down the pier. The fire from the Japanese emplacements was still so heavy that the gunners had to dismantle their weapons and wade ashore with them.

By 1800 the Marines controlled the beach from a point 300 yards west of the pier to the short Burns Philp wharf 400 yards east, and to an average depth of 300 yards — about halfway across the island. At the butt end of beach Red One was a second beach-head, held by a force led by Major Michael Ryan and comprising units from the various battalions which happened to be stranded there. During the

night, half the Marines who had survived stood guard while the rest slept in improvised foxholes.

On the Japanese side, half the garrison of 4,800 men had been killed. The early morning naval bombardment had broken their communications, and Rear Adm. Shibasaki had been unable to control units outside his command post. The only part of the island where he could have found troops for a counter-attack was under almost continual bombardment by the destroyers.

During the night there was intense activity on both sides. Groups of Japanese tried to infiltrate the American perimeters, but they were driven off or wiped out. Several Japanese swam out and occupied a freighter hulk grounded north-west of the pier. Others crawled into disabled tanks and amtracs stranded on the reef. Still others set up machine-guns in the wooden latrines that extended out over the lagoon. The Marines, meanwhile, extended their hold on the island, and landing craft in the lagoon were gradually sorted out and brought under control by Captain John McGovern, who had set up a command post aboard *Pursuit.*

Help from carrier planes

D-plus one, 21 November, opened with the 1st Battalion, 8th Marines fighting their way ashore after 20 hours in their boats. The first three waves hit the centre of the reef and their ramps came down, only to be raked by fire from the nearby hulk occupied by the Japanese during the night. Help came from patrolling carrier planes, which swept down to attack the hulk with bombs and cannon.

But elsewhere the Japanese fire seemed undiminished. They continued to sweep the reef with crossfire from many positions. Marines trying to wade ashore were shot down almost to a man. In fact, during the next few hours the losses the reserve force suffered were greater than those of any battalion landed the previous day.

For Col. Shoup, still operating from his sand-hole command post by an enemy-held shelter, things were not moving fast enough. But radio communications were better this morning and signals flashed from him:

To the Assistant Divisional Commander:
IMPERATIVE YOU GET ALL TYPES AMMUNITION TO ALL LANDING PARTIES IMMEDIATELY.

To *Maryland:*
IMPERATIVE YOU LAND AMMUNITION, WATER, RATIONS AND MEDICAL SUPPLIES IN AMTRACS TO BEACH RED TWO AND EVACUATE CASUALTIES.

Chaos still reigned in the lagoon, with amtracs and boats milling around, their radios and drivers knocked out. Capt. McGovern, transport group commander, on *Pursuit,* using a bullhorn, bellowed out orders and gradually got the situation under control. But troops who attempted to land on beach Red One were driven back to their boats by heavy ground fire, and Col. Shoup reported to Gen. Julian Smith:
SITUATION NOT GOOD.

Then at noon came the break the Marines needed. The tide came up at last and men and machines streamed ashore. With the help of call-fire from the destroyers, Maj. Ryan's men broke out of their narrow beach-head and over-ran three 80mm coast defense guns which had commanded the beach approaches and wrought appalling damage on amtracs and tanks. At 1225 they had reached the southwest corner of the island.

Marines were now landing on the southern half of Green Beach and advancing towards the western end of the air strip. Amtracs went in first, clearing the way for landing craft, and hauled two broken-down tanks off the beach. Maj. Ryan's men held the beach-head while the 1st Battalion, 6th Regiment, landed and dug themselves in, then called for aircraft to bomb the Japanese positions along the southern shore.

By 1700, survivors of the fragmented forces landed on Red Beach Two had fought their way across the airfield and established a small perimeter on the southern shore of the

◁ *This scene on beach Red Two the day after the landing shows in how confined a space the Marines had to fight their way ashore — and what an inviting target they presented. Jammed in a narrow strip are both types of amtrac, a jeep, two 75mm howitzers and a clutter of other equipment. Casualties on this beach were heavy.*
▷ *The cratered surface of Betio's airstrip after bombing and naval gunfire. Palm trees still stand close to some of the large craters — proof of the ability of sand and coral to absorb the blast of even the heaviest bombs. 'Seabees' had the airstrip operational again within days.*

Robert Hunt Library/U.S. Marine Corps

island. Light tanks, which had landed at high water, came rumbling up the beach firing high-explosive shells through the slits of pillboxes and bombproof shelters.

Meanwhile, the 6th Regiment had taken a neighboring island, Batriki, from which they were able to shell Japanese positions on Betio. At 1600, Col. Shoup was able to signal :
WE ARE WINNING.

The enemy force had been split, and the two beach-heads were expanded as position after position was overrun. Urgently wanted medical supplies were brought in and casualties evacuated by a shuttle service of LVTs.

At 1803, the first two jeeps came rolling along the pier towing 37mm guns, and Colonel Merritt Edson, Gen. Julian Smith's chief of staff, arrived to take command of all troops.

Early next morning, 22 November, the Japanese radio on Tarawa sent out its last message :
OUR WEAPONS HAVE BEEN DESTROYED AND FROM NOW ON EVERYONE IS ATTEMPTING A FINAL CHARGE. MAY JAPAN LIVE FOR TEN THOUSAND YEARS.

Desperate enemy resistance

In spite of the hopelessness of their position, the enemy resistance remained desperate all through the day. Light tanks rolled ashore on Beach Green and attacked along the south shore, pouring shellfire into the embrasures of pillboxes and bombshelters whose occupants refused to surrender. Marines followed with grenades and blocks of TNT. Flame-throwers scorched out what resistance was left. By nightfall the Americans had established themselves between the south shore and the east end of the airfield. The only strongpoint at the western end still in Japanese hands was a big bombproof emplacement between Beaches Red One and Red Two.

The 1st Battalion, under Major William Jones, had taken up positions on the eastern end late in the evening. Three times that night the Japanese made fanatical counter-attacks. But the Marines hung on desperately repulsing the attacks with artillery, machine-gun and rifle fire, hand grenades and bayonets, while destroyers *Schroeder* and

Sigsbee pounded at the areas still under enemy control.

On the fourth day, 23 November, the 3rd Battalion, 6th Regiment relieved Maj. Jones's tired troops and swept down the narrow 'barrel' of Betio, systematically wiping out pockets of Japanese. Another team stormed the big bombproof shelter that no naval shell had been able to penetrate, hitting it with TNT, flame-throwers and heavy guns. When they smashed their way into its concrete caverns they found every man dead.

At noon Gen. Julian Smith signalled to Gen. Holland Smith aboard *Pennsylvania,* off Makin :
COMPLETE ANNIHILATION OF ENEMY THIS DATE.

Aftermath

By early afternoon, Marine engineers and Seabees were repairing the airstrip. The invasion of Tarawa had been accomplished. Betio was 'an abomination of desolation', its trees scorched and shredded, its air foul with the smell of scorched and rotting bodies.

The battle for Betio cost the Americans 3,000 dead and wounded — and the Japanese their entire garrison. The Marines took only a few prisoners. The rest, including Rear Adm. Shibasaki, died to a man.

The Marines' casualty figures stunned the US public. Whether the tiny island was worth 1,000 lives has been disputed, but the American forces did gain some notable advantages. Punishing air raids on the Marshalls and Carolines, and reconnaissance flights over a wider area, were mounted from Betio's airstrip. And important lessons in assault landing techniques were also learned — notably the importance of pin-point bombing attacks on specific targets, rather than 'carpet' bombing over an area whose soft sand simply absorbed the shock of the bombs. So the cost of 'bloody Tarawa' was repaid by the lives it saved in later, larger invasions.

Burton Graham

BIAK

Honeycombed with caves, a natural fortress defended by 11,400 Japanese and tanks. But America needed the airfield

Biak Island, the largest of the SW Pacific Schouten Islands, lies across Geelvink Bay on the northern coast of Dutch New Guinea, now Irian Barat, a province of Indonesia. A large island containing three airfields, Biak was vital to General Douglas MacArthur's 1944 return to the Philippines, and the gruelling battle for its possession featured the first tank v. tank battle of the Pacific War.

As a result of the August 1943 Quebec Conference, Gen. MacArthur was directed to isolate—not seize—the formidable Japanese bases at Rabaul and Kavieng in New Britain, and, instead, to capture Manus, in the Admiralty Islands. He was then to leap-frog along the north coast of New Guinea to the Vogelkop Peninsula of Dutch New Guinea, and reach Mindanao by the end of 1944 to begin the reconquest of the Philippines. Sattelberg, Finschhafen (2 October 1943) and Saidor (2 January 1944) were taken in quick Australian and American actions. Then 3rd New Zealand Division seized Green Island on 15 February. A fortnight later, American and Australian units landed on Manus, then Emerau Island (20 March), midway between Kavieng and Manus, bypassing Wewak and Hansa Bay.

While the fighting in Bougainville, New Guinea and the Admiralties went on, MacArthur was directed to seize Aitape and Hollandia (mod. Djajapura), and be ready to invade the Philippines on 15 November. Meanwhile, in the Central Pacific, Admiral Chester W. Nimitz was to seize Saipan, Tinian and Guam islands in the Marianas. Then in mid-September he would secure bases in the Palaus in time to cover MacArthur's advance to the Philippines.

The island-hopping strategy continued with simultaneous landings at Aitape and Hollandia, 120 miles apart, on 22 April. This bypassed over 200,000 Japanese who were now out of the war for the duration. Tiny Wakde Island, 125 miles NW of Hollandia, was next, for it contained a valuable airfield. It was assaulted on 17 May; the 800-strong Japanese garrison was wiped out.

The hold on Manus, Hollandia and Wakde was quickly consolidated. Airfields were rapidly brought into service from which American and Australian aircraft could begin softening up the next target—Biak Island. Its three airstrips were needed to give additional air support to the invasion of Saipan, 1,250 miles away, scheduled for 15 June. MacArthur was directed to have heavy long-range bombers operating from Biak by that date. This was optimistic but then US engineers had prepared usable landing strips at Aitape in two days and only Biak could comfortably operate the B24 Liberator.

Biak is about 45 miles long and 20 wide. Low, flat-topped hills support a thick jungle growth, and there are no natural harbors. The coastline is fringed with a coral reef which extends out for hundreds of yards. Photo-reconnaissance and intelligence reports had shown Bosnik, an enemy supply base on the SE coast, opposite the Padaido Islands, to be well defended. The Bosnik harbor facilities included two stone jetties built across the reef out to deep water. A string of administrative buildings and installations was protected by a coral reef which rose about 200ft to a flat escarpment that stretched nine miles along the southern shore to a mile west of Mokmer. There it swung north, leaving a flat coastal plain on which the Japanese had built three airstrips and a

US Army

◁△ *A knocked-out Japanese Type 95 light tank lies amid shattered palms on a beach between Bosnik and Mokmer airfield, Biak, 26 June, 1944.*
△ *Ten days before the assault on Biak, the small island of Wadke was taken as part of the US island-hopping strategy towards Japan. Here men of the 163rd US Infantry Regiment 41st Division, hit the beach from Higgins boats. On 31 May they joined the attack on Biak.*

coastal road. Remembering particularly the high cost in lives of the bloody November 1943 Tarawa Marine landing (see 'War Monthly' Issue 1), the American planners were reluctant to risk a landing across the coral, even using LVT, 'amtracs'. Bosnik was chosen because its jetties looked usable and because, not backed by swamps, it offered firm ground behind the beaches for dispersal and maneuver.

Biak was a natural fort. Behind the first ridge, there were not only caves and raw upjutting coral cliffs, but also deep ravines and thick tangled jungle. The limestone caves about 1,200 yards north of the western end of the Mokmer airstrip were the key to the defense and cavernous enough to hold a thousand men. Another series of caves ran under the main ridge north of Mokmer village, and a third honeycombed the jagged jungle-covered ridges west of the Parai Defile.

It was generally believed that Biak was lightly held, by 'not more than 2,000 Japanese'. But the garrison totalled 11,400 men. Of these at least 4,000 were seasoned combat troops, including the crack 222nd Infantry Regiment which comprised 3,400 veterans of the China war sent in December 1943. There were numerous service and supply units

including three airfield construction battalions. Other elements included a light tank company with at least 12 tanks; 19th Naval Guard Unit (125 men); and 28th Naval Special Base Force of 1,500 men.

Lieutenant General Takuzo Numata, chief of staff to the Second Area Army commander, was on a visit to Biak and took over command from Colonel Nasyiki Kuzume, commander of the 222nd. Numata prepared for the worst. He and Col. Kuzume expected the enemy to land near Mokmer airstrip, and concentrated their defenses around it. Four 4.7in naval dual-purpose guns and one 6in coast defense gun were undamaged. Field and AA guns of up to 90mm calibre and numerous mortars and automatic weapons were located on the coral terrace and on a spur ridge behind Mokmer village. This position straddling a 240ft height was less than 800 yards from the sea while the HQ West Caves region, studded with bunkers and pillboxes, could keep the runways under fire from anything heavier than a rifle.

The approaching *Hurricane* Task Force comprised two regiments of 41st United States Infantry Division under its commander, Major-General Horace H. Fuller. Rear Admiral William M. Fechteler was Commander, Attack Force. He led five cruisers and 21 destroyers escorting 36 transports and large landing craft. Engineering equipment would be needed in the early stages of landing for the construction of beaching points. Conventional landing craft could not be used because of the 200-yard width of coral reef confronting the Bosnik beaches. Fechteler and Fuller decided to use six LSTs to tow in the initial assault force. This would comprise 63 LVTs manned by troops of the 542nd Engineer Boat and

Shore Regiment and 25 DUKW amphibious lorries carrying an army motor transport company. The LSTs would also tow eight LCTs containing tanks, artillery and engineering equipment. The bulk of the 41st Division would follow in 15 LCTs, which could use the jetties. Z-day had been set for 27 May.

The invasion force left Humboldt Bay, Hollandia, on the evening of 25 May steering direct for Biak, 320 miles distant, at a sedate 8.5-knot towing speed. Dawn on the 27th broke to ideal landing conditions : the sky overcast and breathless, the sea a dead grey calm. At 0629 the Allied attack force was in position, standing off Bosnik. Rear Adm. Fechteler gave the order : EXECUTE LANDING PLAN.

Immediately, the US light cruisers *Phoenix*, *Boise* and *Nashville*, standing broadside on, opened fire with their 45 6in guns, hitting shore installations over 12 miles of coast from Sorido airstrip to east of Bosnik. Australian heavy cruisers *Shropshire* and *Australia* laid on 400 rounds of 8in. Overhead, 37 Liberators, in two waves, pattern-bombed the shore defenses. As the smoke and dust of the 45-minute bombardment drifted seaward, visibility fell to 500 yards. Two rocket-armed LCIs took up positions, one on each flank of the leading wave of amtracs, to lay down a last-minute 5in rocket blanket barrage as the troops approached the beach. A breeze-created haze obscured all landmarks.

Visibility was zero as the first wave of 16 LVTs hit the beach at 0719, to find itself in a mangrove swamp about 3,000 yards west of Beach Green 4. As the 32 amtracs of the second and third waves, and the 25 DUKWs of the fourth and fifth waves, crept slowly shoreward, they made the same error. The entire formation had drifted westward in a 3-knot current. The first four waves, comprising 2nd Battalion, 186th Infantry Regiment, were safely ashore, if in the wrong place, and by 0730 were pushing through the mangroves to the main coastal road. The last wave of DUKWs carrying 3rd Battalion, 186th Infantry, landed 800 yards to the east.

'No' to change of plan

Colonel Oliver P. Newman, commanding 186th Infantry, was supposed to secure the beach-head. He suggested at 0746 that his misplaced regiment exchange missions with 162nd Regiment, the follow-up force in 15 LCIs whose task was to drive rapidly west and capture the Mokmer airstrip. But Maj. Gen. Fuller refused to change the plan. The two regiments had to pass each other to reach their assigned positions and the unravelling took an hour and a half.

The jetties, found by radar, were in good condition. There was still no opposition, and the landing went on as planned in a way almost too good to be true. Some LCTs were unloaded at the eastern jetty, and others found suitable beaching points. Four LSTs tied up at the west jetty, while three others were unloaded by landing craft.

Between 1103 and 1150, 77 Liberators came over in high-level pattern-bombing runs, pounding the airfields and shore installations. As the cloud cover broke up, B25 Mitchell and Douglas A20 Havoc medium bombers appeared and patrolled ready for call strikes. And now P40 Kittyhawks and P38 Lightnings arrived to provide fighter-cover.

By the afternoon, everything was under control, and the LSTs went on discharging their cargoes without interruption. All day 542nd Engineer Boat and Shore Regiment prepared exits and entrances, built protected supply and ammunition dumps, and bulldozed a network of roads. They

placed two pontoon sections on the reef near the east jetty for use as beaching points.

Two ineffectual afternoon raids by six Japanese planes apart, there had been no air or sea opposition. Ashore it looked as if it might be a walkover. During the afternoon, all Z-day objectives were taken. By 1715, 12,000 troops, 12 tanks, 29 artillery pieces, 500 vehicles and 2,400 tons of supplies had been unloaded. Only 300 tons of equipment remained aboard the LSTs when they withdrew at the end of the day. At 1800, Rear Adm. Fechteler left Biak with the LST formation, leaving two destroyers and the rocket LCIs to provide gunfire support for the ground troops.

The progress made on this Z-day had greatly exceeded expectations. The landing had been carried out and the beaches secured more cheaply with less confusion and congestion than in any previous New Guinea operation. By dark, the troops had dug in around Parai village, having been delayed briefly at the defile, but well pleased with their five-mile tank-supported advance.

Early on 28 May the 162nd Infantry continued its push toward Mokmer airfield. By 0930 it had reached the road junction 200 yards east of the field; that was as close as the Americans would get for the next nine days. Behind the first ridge there were not only caves and raw upjutting coral cliffs, but also deep ravines and tangled jungle. From hidden positions, the Japanese were able to bring to bear heavy plunging MG and mortar fire. The 2nd Battalion of 222nd Regiment threw the 3/162nd back 600 yards, then with a well-timed attack from the north cut off the US unit from 2nd Battalion in Mokmer village. At 1400 Japanese light tanks actually started moving down the airfield to stiffen a third assault. Destroyers and 3rd Platoon, 603rd Tank Company, shooting 1,200 yards, forced them back to hull-down positions, but three US tanks were hit by Japanese artillery. Ordered to fall back at 1600, the 3/162nd took two hours to extricate itself and minus 103 men rejoined 2nd Battalion back in their Z-day position. Patchy naval and air support hampered by poor shore links, had failed to reduce the volume of Japanese fire.

At 0700 on the 29th two Japanese battalions resumed the onslaught. An hour later, four Type 95 (1935) light tanks deployed ahead of an infantry column in a coconut grove between the beach and cliffs. Two Sherman M4A1 medium tanks promptly engaged them. It was an unequal duel for the American 75mm guns could have penetrated all four of their opponents together, even if they had been lined up nose to tail 2,000 yards away. As it was, the 75mm AP shot went clean through the 12mm plate of each one. Then the US gunners ably switched to pumping HE shells into their hapless foes. These shattered the stationary wrecks and blew their turrets right off. The puny Japanese 37mm guns did score hits but had no chance of penetrating the Sherman's 3in (76mm) frontal armor.

Half an hour later three more Type 95s met their end in the coconut grove underlining the chronic disparity in tank technology and training. One 37mm hit jammed a Sherman's gun-barrel, but the resourceful American crew reversed their tank into a shell crater and destroyed their adversary at the elevation dictated. Nevertheless, after midday, the Japanese infantry, using their classic infiltration tactics, set up a roadblock east of Parai. The US reserves soon cleared it, but Colonel Harold Haney of 162nd Infantry was persuaded of the need to retreat.

The Americans were partly forced to evacuate by sea, a rarity for their brand of amphibious warfare. During the

US Army

△ Troops of Company A,
(1st Battalion) 186th
US Infantry Regiment
accompanied by a Sherman
tank, making their way
through shelled jungle to
the north of Mokmer
airstrip, Biak, on 17 June
1944. Their mission was
the elimination of pockets
of Japanese resistance in
the West Caves. The
Japanese forces in the
caves made a few sporadic
attempts to come out and
harass the US infantry,
but flamethrowers,
grenades, drums of petrol,
plus two 500lb charges of
TNT detonated in the caves
by a demolition detail,
proved too much.
▷ Keeping their heads
well down out of small
arms fire troops of the
163rd Inf Regt, 41st Div,
crowd onto a Wadke beach.
Their experience was to be
repeated at Biak and other
islands.

US Army

49

afternoon, all available landing craft were pressed into service to take half the 162nd off the beach at Parai. The troops were delivered back on land just before nightfall, about 500 yards west of Ibdi village. Two battalions with the tanks and artillery got through by road, but first had to destroy several heavy mortars. They had been forced back two miles with a loss of 115 men in the day and the Japanese pursued closely despite much heavier casualties.

By now, Maj. Gen. Fuller had realized that the Biak airfields would never be taken until the Japanese had been cleared from the high ground. He planned to attack along the ridge behind Bosnik. He signalled for five more battalions of all arms. While waiting for two battalions of 163rd Infantry from Wakde, Fuller was content to halt the 162nd except for patrolling up to the inland plateau. He assembled all AA weapons destined for defense of the Biak airfields along the beach in preparation for enemy air attacks.

The 16 LCIs carrying the remainder of 41st Division arrived at 1300 on 31 May, and during the afternoon the troops were successfully landed with gunfire support from the sea. On the following morning, the 186th Infantry began to advance westward along the inland plateau hampered more by the lack of water than Japanese. The 162nd fought its way along the coast. On 2 June, neighboring Owi and Mios Woendi islands were occupied, and Army Engineers began the construction of an airstrip on Owi, while Mios Woendi was turned into a seaplane, patrol boat and amphibious repair base. It was plain that the island would be more difficult to capture than anyone had envisaged, and that estimates of Japanese garrison strength and defenses had been wrong.

And now there entered another unexpected factor—Operation *A-Go*, introduced by Admiral Soemu Toyoda, new C-in-C of the Japanese Combined Fleet. Its aim was to compensate for Japan's inferiority in ships and aircraft, especially in carriers, by luring the US Pacific Fleet into an area which could be reached by land-based aircraft. Toyoda saw the loss of Biak's airfields as a threat to his plans and immediately ordered the island to be reinforced. Aircraft were rushed to western New Guinea from Japan and the Central Pacific. Bombers from the Halmaheras raided Wakde and destroyed over 60 planes on the ground. Meanwhile, Toyoda assembled his forces in the Tawi Tawi-Davao-Halmahera area for Operation *Kon*—the relief of Biak—in preparation for which 23rd Naval Air Flotilla was strengthened by 166 planes.

Hurried preparations were made to transport 2,500 troops of 2nd Amphibious Brigade from Mindanao escorted by three naval squadrons totalling a battleship, three heavy cruisers, eight destroyers and two minelayers.

It was hoped that this formidable force, aided by an intensive but profitless 2 June air strike which cost 12 aircraft, would get to within striking distance of Biak without being sighted. But on the morning of 3 June, the main force sighted a periscope. Then, before noon, the entire fleet was sighted by a Liberator operating from Wakde. Simultaneously, a Japanese search plane reported Allied naval forces including a carrier at Biak, where there was nothing larger than a destroyer. The convoy was ordered to turn back. Had it reached Biak, the troops could have landed without difficulty and the warships would have created havoc by bombarding the beach-head and destroying the shipping.

The *Kon* operation was not abandoned immediately, but the Japanese ships were now on the run from Allied planes and submarines. In a second attempt to reach Biak on 8 June, their ships were struck by 10 B25s, which sank one destroyer and damaged three others. Five destroyers pushed on for the island, but a superior US-Australian covering squadron saw them off in a three-hour stern-chase. One Japanese destroyer was hit in the 35-knot night action fought at ranges of never less than eight miles. A third attempt, involving the super-battleships *Yamato* and *Musashi*, was called off on 12 June when the US Fifth Fleet's appearance in the Philippine sea attracted all major Combined Fleet units north. Yet, though the Japanese lost a number of ships and several barges filled with troops, they

△▷ *Route of the long, inexorable US drive to the ultimate conquest of the Philippines.*

◁ *Usually seen at sea during assault landings, this amtrac, still with its guns at the ready, is crawling around Biak's shell-torn beaches on 9 June 1944.*

▷ *The DUKW, an amphibious six-wheeled 2½-ton 'sea lorry', first used in March 1943, for short-haul delivery of men and equipment from ship to shore. During 1942-45 21,247 'Ducks' were built in US plants.*

Australian War Memorial

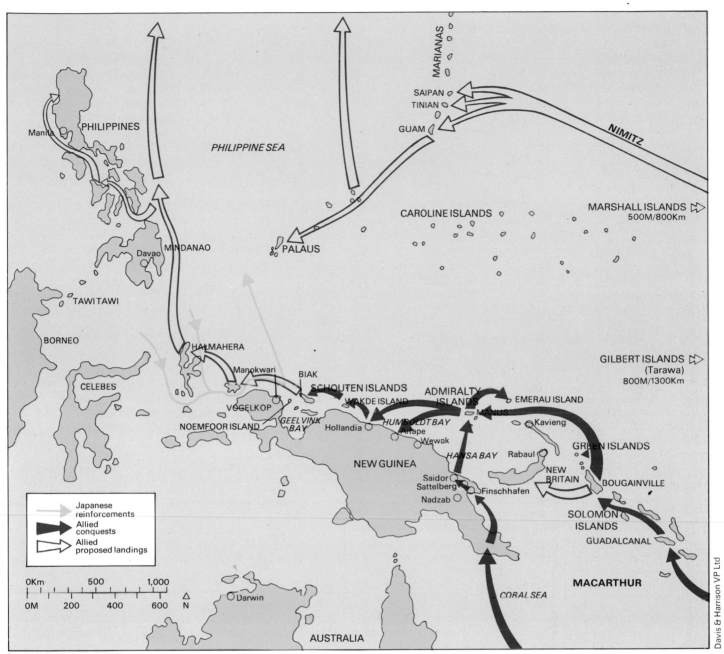

Japanese reinforcements

Allied conquests

Allied proposed landings

MARIANAS

SAIPAN
TINIAN
GUAM

NIMITZ

PHILIPPINES

Manila

PHILIPPINE SEA

MARSHALL ISLANDS
500M/800Km

CAROLINE ISLANDS

MINDANAO

Davao

PALAUS

TAWI TAWI

BORNEO

GILBERT ISLANDS
(Tarawa)
800M/1300Km

HALMAHERA

CELEBES

Manokwari   BIAK

SCHOUTEN ISLANDS

WAKDE ISLAND

ADMIRALTY ISLANDS

MANUS

EMERAU ISLAND

VOGELKOP

GEEL VINK BAY

Hollandia

NOEMFOOR ISLAND

HUMBOLDT BAY

Aitape

Wewak

Kavieng

GREEN ISLANDS

NEW GUINEA

HANSA BAY

Rabaul

NEW BRITAIN

BOUGAINVILLE

Saidor
Sattelberg
Nadzab

Finschhafen

SOLOMON ISLANDS

GUADALCANAL

MACARTHUR

CORAL SEA

0Km   500   1,000
0M   200   400   600   N

Darwin

AUSTRALIA

Davis & Harrison VP Ltd

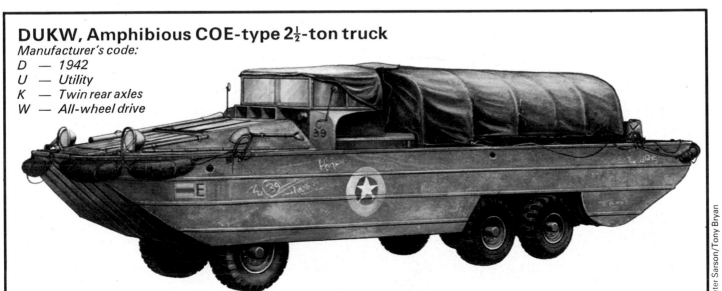

DUKW, Amphibious COE-type 2½-ton truck

Manufacturer's code:

D — 1942
U — Utility
K — Twin rear axles
W — All-wheel drive

Peter Sarson/Tony Bryan

Japanese Type 95 Light Tank

Weight 7.4 tons
Crew 3
Armament 1 37mm Type 97, 300 rnds
2 7.7mm MG Type 97, 2,970 rnds
Engine 6-cyl ohv air-cooled diesel; 110hp at 1,400rpm

Steering Brake and clutch
Speed 25mph
Range 150 miles
Armor 6-14mm
Length 14ft 4in
Height 7ft
Width 6ft 9in

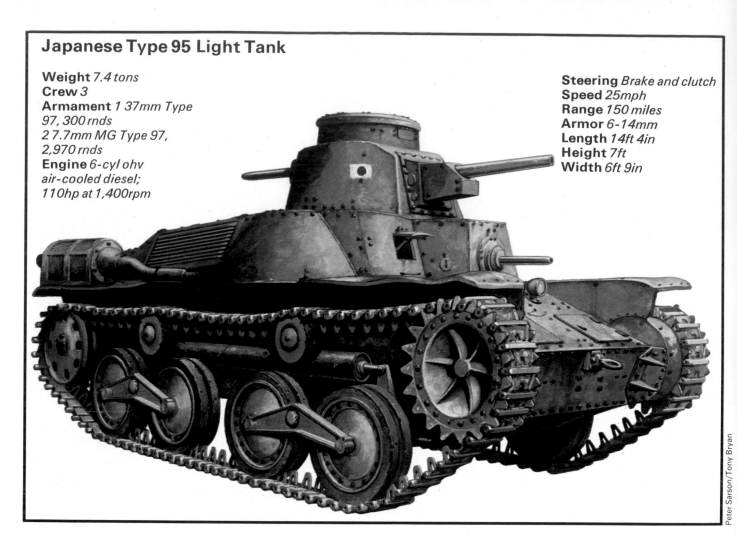

Peter Sarson/Tony Bryan

still managed to reinforce the Biak garrison by 1,200 men mainly from Manokwari on the Vogelkop Peninsula via neighboring Noemfoor Island.

With these reinforcements coming in, the Americans were making little or no progress. The caves and tunnels under the cliffs and the jungle made it impossible to find the major caverns which hid the main enemy forces and many of their mortar and mountain batteries. The caves had connecting corridors and exits which permitted the defenders literally to disappear from the face of the earth, then reappear in the midst of the invaders. On 7 June 186th Infantry plunged down into the coastal plain from the inland plateau seizing Mokmer airfield after their full-scale artillery preparation and two-battalion attack fell on undefended ground. A golden opportunity to take the Japanese positions from inland had been lost. And now the Americans found themselves ringed by the fire of Biak's strongest positions and pinned down much as they had been on 28-29 May; the only differences being that no costly Japanese counter-attack was attempted and tenuous US supply was possible at night across the Mokmer beaches. Two LCMs with their ramps jammed by enemy hits had to return the 9½ miles to Bosnik in reverse.

Eventually on 10 June the Mokmer perimeter was linked up to 162nd Infantry pushing through Parai for the second time. On 13 June the first US aircraft landed at Mokmer but the field was still under harassing fire that made its regular use impossible. The Americans were also beset by other troubles. An epidemic of scrub typhus had broken out on Owi Island and spread to Biak. Stringent measures had to

be introduced to keep the infestation in check and to get the troops back to combat fitness. The entire operation was now running far behind schedule. After chivying from MacArthur, who had publicly announced victory on Biak, Maj. Gen. Fuller was replaced by Lieutenant General Robert L. Eichelberger on 15 June.

Lt. Gen. Numata left the island in a seaplane from Korim Bay on 15 June, after ordering Col. Kuzume to prolong the defense for as long as possible. The dwindling garrison was to obey, holding on with almost inhuman tenacity. They even managed two spoiling attacks on 15 June using five tanks. It was a better day for Japanese armor. Unopposed by Shermans and opening fire at 250 yards, they inflicted considerable losses on US infantry but lost two of their number to bazookas and a third to .50 Browning MG fire.

As the days dragged on past the date on which MacArthur had wanted bombers flying from Biak in support of the Saipan invasion, the hard, relentless slogging went on. The caves had to be reduced one by one, using flame-throwers, ignited petrol and even electrically fired 500lb charges of TNT. In many cases the only solution was to seal the entrances and exits, leaving the Japanese to suffocate or die of starvation. On 18 June a fourth US infantry regiment joined the fray, but the original invaders were still hard at it. Col. Kuzume's stubborn and heroic defense denied the Americans use of Mokmer airfield until 20 June, when the engineers were able to restart work. The other two airstrips, Borokoe and Sorido, were captured on the same day, and two days later the first fighters landed on Mokmer. The fighter strip on Owi had been completed, and two squadrons

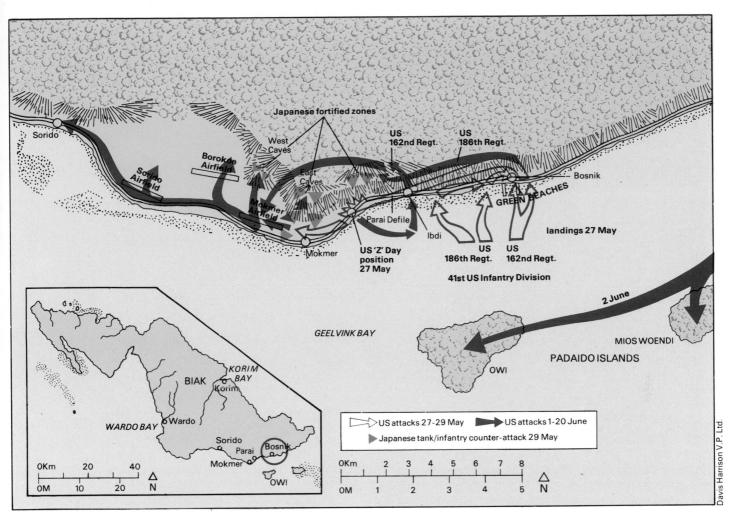

Legend:
US attacks 27-29 May — US attacks 1-20 June
Japanese tank/infantry counter-attack 29 May

The US Army assault on Biak island, 180 miles NW of Wadke, began on 27 May 1944. Objectives were airfields at Borokde, Mokmer and Sorido, essential for continuing air-strikes along the island chain and the replenishment of stores and equipment. First landings were made on Green beaches 1 to 4 in the Bosnik area. Organized resistance ceased on 22 June, although even on 17 August Japan's 2nd Batt. 222nd Infantry were trying to organize themselves into a final counter-attack state.

flew in on 22 June.

On the morning of 22 June, the bitter siege of Biak was effectively over. Col. Kuzume burned his regimental colours then committed *hara-kiri*. The West Caves were a charnel house by the time the Americans finished scouring them out on 27 June. The East Caves garrison melted away into the interior before 3 July. But the thousand Ibdi Pocket defenders fought to a finish against everything American ingenuity and firepower could do for more than a month, until 22 July. It took 155mm shells and 1,000lb bombs to paralyze the last defenders who clung to some of the 75 four-man coral-and-log pillboxes. It was pointless and wasteful resistance, the gesture of Oriental militarism against Western technology. Mopping up lasted another month, officially until 20 August, with two small subsidiary landings on Korim and Wardo bays.

As was almost invariably the case, Japanese deaths exceeded all Allied battle casualties combined because of the 'resistance-while-breath-remained' philosophy that had to be fulfilled regardless of circumstances. Nevertheless the

ratio was more favorable than usual to Japan because of US losses from disease which totalled 6,811. Many of these men were *hors de combat* for several months, but only seven deaths resulted from 1,000 scrub typhus cases. US deaths in action by sea and land totalled 471 with 2,443 wounded. The three infantry regiments of 41st Division lost very heavily, 2,025 men or a third of their strength with 162nd Infantry losing 933. They had killed 4,700 Japanese, captured 220 and released 600 slave laborers. By early October starvation and attrition had raised the first two figures to 6,125 and 765.

With hindsight, from the Allied point of view, Biak was well worth the cost. American aircraft were able to use the three airfields in great numbers, and the base, supporting 70,000 men, became an important stepping-stone in MacArthur's island-hopping campaign. But Biak had been of most benefit to the Allies while its conquest was incomplete. It had drawn Japanese airpower like a magnet away from the Central Pacific; 1st Air Fleet had only a fifth of the planes intended to strike at the US fleet in the Philippine Sea. The Biak relief attempts had so disrupted and delayed Japanese naval movements that there was even less co-ordination than usual between their sea and land-based airpower. The outcome was an unmitigated defeat by 22 June in which Japan lost nearly 500 aircraft and about 450 even more irreplaceable pilots. This was pure gain, more than outweighing the delay imposed on an over-optimistic timetable for using airfields on one more captured Pacific island.

Burton Graham

IWO JIMA

A fortress of volcanic ash and rock. It claimed the lives of over 20,000 Japanese and 6,000 US Marines

Marines of 5th Division pinned down in the volcanic ash of their landing beach on the morning of 19 February 1945. Four days would pass before Mt. Suribachi (background) fell, 36 before Iwo Jima was taken. Two months mopping-up followed.

Iwo Jima made an unremarked appearance on the island-littered map of the Pacific when, over 50 years ago, an underwater volcano spewed out ash and mud. The eight square miles of barren ash and soft, freshly-formed rock might have remained in obscurity but for the strategic significance of this speck of land in the battle for the Pacific in World War II. Vital to the American campaign of rolling back the newly-acquired Pacific empire of the Japanese to attack the enemy homeland, the grim battle for the tiny island lasted over a month and at the end 5,800 Americans and nearly 22,000 Japanese lay dead. Seizure of the island would deny the Japanese an excellent strategic base and give the Americans a bomber base only 660 nautical miles from Tokyo. Previous bombing missions had flown from the Marianas, 2,800 miles from Japan—a range which precluded fighter escort and led to heavy B29 Superfortress casualties. Iwo Jima was also a necessary link in the air defenses of the Marianas and it had to be captured, not merely isolated. There was a final consideration—the island was traditionally Japanese territory, administered from Tokyo, and its fall would be a severe psychological blow to the enemy.

Such blows were important. The Japanese had expanded their empire at a phenomenal rate. In the first five months of 1942 they had captured territory stretching from Burma in the west, through the Malay archipelago, to the central Pacific island groups of the Gilberts and the Marshalls. Control of these islands, small in size, gave them air command of the surrounding area, and command of the skies was vital to control of the seas.

The Americans responded in two ways. They built up fast carrier-based forces which could gain command of the air

in disputed areas, from which land and sea control could follow. To gain land control they devised sophisticated amphibious assault techniques to capture island bases. The land targets were so small that such invasions were, in reality, direct attacks on fortified positions and the landing was not an orthodox preliminary move, it was the battle itself.

Naval victories at the Coral Sea on 7 May 1942 and a month later at Midway, on 4-5 June, started the American comeback. On 7 August 19,000 Marines under Major General Alexander A. Vandegrift landed on the island of Guadalcanal in the southern Solomons. The move took the local Japanese commanders by surprise and there was no need for an amphibious assault. On the nearby island of Tulagi, however, the Marines had a grim struggle with the local garrison and learned their first lesson—that the Japanese soldier, even if his position was hopeless, would fight to the death rather than surrender.

The next step in the Pacific re-conquest was a two-pronged assault. General Douglas MacArthur thrust into the south-west Pacific, taking the Solomons, isolating Rabaul on the island of New Britain, and 'hopping' along the northern coast of New Guinea. Admiral Chester W. Nimitz's central Pacific forces captured the Gilbert, Marshall and Mariana groups, and isolated the Carolines. So swift was the American drive that on 20 October 1944 the re-conquest of the Philippines began, against which the Japanese could offer only sporadic resistance after their naval defeat at Leyte Gulf.

The US Marines played a decisive part in the drive across the Pacific, particularly in the central Pacific advance. In their first attack, against the Gilbert Islands in November

The assault waves hit the beach. Seven Marine battalions had a 30-minute, 4,000-yard ride to the shore in 482 amphibious tractors. Ten destroyers, 50 gunboats, rocket craft and mortar vessels gave close-support fire all the way in.

1943, the Corps suffered heavy losses in the confused and bloody assault on Tarawa. Yet they learned a lot from the assault and in later and larger operations in the Marshalls and Marianas the benefits of earlier experience were clearly revealed. Now, at the beginning of 1945, with Japan pushed almost back to her national boundaries, the Marines were preparing for their toughest assignment yet—the assault on Iwo Jima.

The Japanese were also aware of Iwo Jima's importance and began speedy reinforcement towards the end of 1944. A garrison of 23,000 men under Lieutenant General Tadamichi Kuribayashi was sent to the island with orders to hold out as long as possible—American air and naval superiority ruled out further reinforcement. Kuribayashi was a courageous and dedicated soldier, described by Tokyo Radio as one whose 'partly protruding belly is packed full of strong fighting spirit'.

The Japanese took with them 120 big guns of over 75mm calibre, 300 anti-aircraft guns of over 25mm, 20,000 small guns, including machine-guns, 130 8cm and 12cm howitzers, 20 20cm mortars, 70 20cm rocket-guns, 40 47mm and 20 37mm anti-tank guns, and 27 tanks. The building of pillboxes began in October 1944 and five months later 360 were complete. A superb network of deep, interconnected caves, which were almost impervious to naval bombardment, was built. All this on an island of eight square miles.

Adm. Nimitz entrusted overall control of the Iwo Jima operation to Admiral Raymond Spruance's Fifth Fleet which, with its fast carrier and battleship units supported by a mobile fleet train, was the most powerful naval body in the world. Its role was to give distant cover against enemy air or naval attack and to participate in the bombardment of the island. Rear Admiral Richmond Kelly Turner, probably the most experienced leader of amphibious operations in World War II, was given command of the landings. The assault troops, 84,000 in all, were to come from 4th and 5th Marine Divisions, with 3rd Marine Division in floating reserve, of Major General Harry Schmidt's 5th Marine Amphibious Corps.

Major General Groves B. Erskine's 3rd Division had fought at Guam and Bougainville and the 4th Division, under Major General Clifton B. Cates, had seen action at Roi-Namur, Saipan and Tinian. Major General Keller E. Rockey's 5th Division did not have combat experience but they were well trained and strengthened by many veterans. Lieutenant General 'Howlin' Mad' Smith, the vigorous leader of the 1st Marine Division at Guadalcanal and now commander of the Fleet Marine Force, Pacific, was placed in an intermediate position between Spruance and Schmidt. With such a well-tried team of commanders and good calibre soldiers there was little doubt about the eventual outcome of the operation. The question was, how easy—or difficult—would the Marines find the assault?

From late 1944 the most intensive softening up process yet of the Pacific War began. Army bombers flew by day, Marine ones by night with ever-increasing intensity in the weeks leading up to the invasion, which was scheduled for 19 February 1945. Three days before the landings, Rear Admiral William Blandy's Amphibious Support Force, which included five battleships, began an intensive bombardment of the island. At the same time, Spruance supervised the fast carrier forces in their aerial attacks on Honshu to neutralize any possible Japanese air strikes against the Iwo Jima invasion fleet.

The shelling of Iwo Jima proved completely inadequate, as Schmidt had forecast in repeated requests for a longer, 10-day bombardment. The Americans received a shock on 17 February when 11 of 12 gunboats supporting beach demolition teams were sunk by enemy fire. Blandy realized from this that the island's defenses were far heavier than had been expected and accepted Schmidt's advice to concentrate bombardment on the beaches and nearby areas. Iwo Jima, like Tarawa, was so small that it was virtually all beach—unless enemy fire could be neutralized before the assault the Marines would be completely exposed.

The 'gunboat incident' benefited the Americans in two ways. It forced a reassessment of the enemy defenses and also exposed many Japanese gun positions. It seems unlikely that the orders to open fire came from high-ranking commanders—the first of Kuribayashi's 'Essential Battle Instructions' demanded that 'while the enemy bombardment is going on, we must take cover in the dugouts and we must keep our casualties to a minimum'. Kuribayashi was swift to order redeployment of the guns that had opened fire.

With a broad rocky plateau in the north and the extinct volcano of Mount Suribachi at the southern tip of the pork-chop shaped island of Iwo Jima, the only place a full-scale invasion could be mounted was on the black cinder beaches along the south-east coast. From this point it was only a short distance to airfield No. 1; but a landing here also meant that the open beaches would be subjected to an intense fire from higher ground to the north and the south.

At 0640 on 19 February, just before sunrise, Blandy's ships, now reinforced by two battleships and 13 cruisers from Spruance's fleet, opened up with a stupendous close-range bombardment of the island. The astonishing number of 450 ships ringed the island. Blasted by shells ranging from five-inch to 16in in diameter, the beaches seemed to be torn apart. Shortly afterwards, rocket-firing gunboats attacked the Motoyama plateau while other gunboats lobbed mortar rounds at Mount Suribachi. Then, as the firing was temporarily checked and the various ships moved into their final positions, carrier aircraft and heavy bombers from the Marianas showered the areas surrounding the beaches with rockets, napalm and bombs. After a further ten minutes the naval shelling recommenced, joined by ten destroyers and over 50 gunboats which steamed as close inshore as possible in an effort to screen the approaching invasion armada. The whole co-ordinated action was immensely impressive—one history of the battle describes the bombardment as 'a power-laden deployment packing the utmost momentum yet devised by the mind and engineering of man. This was the acme of amphibious assault.'

As the naval bombardment, now a creeping barrage, reached its crescendo, the landing-ships lowered their ramps and the first of the five assault waves emerged, 5,500 yards from the shore. Each wave consisted of 69 amphtracs, armored amphibian tractors which could take 20 troops each right onto the beach and scramble over coral reefs if necessary. The first wave, the 4th Marine Division on the right, the 5th on the left, moved virtually undisturbed towards the shore. At 0902, after 30 minutes' steaming, the amphtracs hit the beach, spewing out their men and the armored mortar and rocket-firing vehicles.

They were immediately up against two unexpected physical obstacles—black volcanic ash into which men sank up to a foot or more, and a steep terrace 15ft high in some places, which only a few amphtracs managed to climb. Most

The Leathernecks storm ashore. These 4th Division Marines are scrambling up an 8ft ash terrace, behind the rolling naval barrage, but their equipment trolleys will have difficulty getting up as did all wheeled and tracked vehicles.

stayed on the beach, getting in the way of oncoming waves, while the troops jumped out and struggled through the ash. One Marine described how he 'tried to sprint up the terrace wall but my feet only bogged in the sand and instead of running I crawled, trying to keep my rifle clean but failing'. Fresh waves of assault troops arrived every five minutes and soon 10,000 men and 400 vehicles were on the beach. Despite inevitable confusion the first combat patrols pushed 150 yards inland, then 300. And then the enemy opened up.

From rabbit-holes, bunkers and pillboxes, small arms and machine-gun fire crashed into the Marines. Heavy artillery and mortars, from deep emplacements and caves on Suribachi and the Motoyama plateau, and trained exactly on the beaches well in advance, thundered out, destroying men and machines. The Japanese garrison, true to their orders, had withheld fire during the landings—only five amphtracs were lost from the early waves. As the momentum of the assault slowed at the terrace and the creeping barrage out-distanced the Marines, the defenders nearest the beach were able to recover and man their weapons. The ash on the beach cushioned all but direct blasts from the mortars and artillery —but one war correspondent stated that 'nowhere . . . have I seen such badly mangled bodies'. It soon became clear that to stay on the beach was near-suicide—but to move off it meant moving into fire from the well-developed defense system.

At this point—and probably only here—the outcome of the battle was in doubt. If the Japanese had mounted a counter-attack, they might have routed the disorganized Marines. But the lessons of Tarawa, Roi-Namur, Saipan and Guam were that furious counter-assaults upon the invaders simply exposed the defenders to the overwhelming American fire-power. Kuribayashi's task was to deny Iwo Jima to the enemy for as long as possible and his troops were ordered to stay strictly on the defensive. Many of the guns were firing only sporadically to conserve their ammunition, although no one at the beach-head would have believed this. The initiative still lay with the Marines—they and their equipment were successfully ashore. Now they could, they *must*, go forward.

Slowly, desperately slowly, the Marines pushed inland, a confused collection of small groups rather than a united force. Each bunker, each rabbit-hole meant a fight to the death. Each enemy position was supported by many others —the Japanese would disappear down one hole and pop up at another, often behind rather than in front of the advancing Marines. The Marines struggled on, pouring bullets, grenades and flame into enemy positions. Flail tanks rumbled forward with the Marines, detonating land mines, tank-dozers carved channels through the terrace and ordinary tanks relieved the pressure on the Marines by knocking out machine-gun nests and pillboxes. But it was no pushover, even with the armor. Facing 4th Division's lines, for example, were ten reinforced concrete blockhouses, seven covered artillery positions and 80 pillboxes. A battalion commander asserted that 'whenever a man showed himself in the lines it was almost certain death'. By mid-afternoon the reserve battalions of four regimental combat teams and two tank battalions had been committed to the battle to relieve the pressure on the leading units.

As dusk fell on this first, bloody day of the campaign, the numbers of Marines had risen to 30,000, with the committal ashore of the reserve regiments for both divisions. On the left flank Colonel Harry B. Liversedge's 28th Regiment had

US Coast Guards assist a blood spattered Marine, wounded when his amtrac took a direct hit. Coast Guard-manned landing craft swiftly evacuated casualties to off-shore LST hospital ships and medical treatment was the best of the Pacific war.

pushed across to the ridge which overlooked the beaches on the south-west; but fierce enemy opposition had halted its progress towards its main target, Mount Suribachi. Next in line was Colonel Thomas A. Wornham's 27th Regiment, which had similarly been brought to a halt in its efforts to overrun airfield No. 1. Farther to the right were the two regiments of the 4th Division, Colonel Walter W. Wensinger's 23rd Marines and Colonel John R. Lanigan's 25th Marines; both had come under extremely heavy fire from the entire Motoyama plateau area, and the 25th Regiment, being farthest on the right, suffered many casualties—one battalion had only 150 men left in the front line.

Although the Marines had failed to reach their first day's objectives, they had secured a foothold and, aided by the inflow of reserves, were digging in to await the expected counter-attack. It didn't come. Instead, the Japanese kept up a deadly accurate mortar and artillery fire against the beaches, causing great damage and loss of life. Most feared of all were the 60 and 250kg bombs which the Japanese had converted into rockets, which came screaming out of the blue to burst upon impact. 'A nightmare in hell' was one description of the scene.

On the second morning, after a 50-minute naval bombardment, the Marines moved on again. But progress was, if anything, even slower than on the previous day. Liversedge's 28th Regiment, making repeated attacks upon the approaches to Mount Suribachi with the aid of artillery, half-tracks and destroyers positioned nearby, advanced only 200 yards that day. To the north the 4th Division reached their objectives on No. 1 airfield and then swung right to face the rising ground that constituted Kuribayashi's first major defense line. Here, too, early progress soon petered out. On the next day this line remained virtually static but the 28th Regiment, again assisted by naval and aerial bombardment, penetrated almost to the foot of Suribachi.

Mountain symbol of mastery

The rugged volcanic mountain, rising steeply out of the sea to a height of 556ft, was not of central importance to the defense of Iwo Jima. Yet it offered fine observation and artillery siting positions and, because of its imposing appearance, control of it tended to symbolize mastery of the island. Recognizing that it would soon be cut off, Kuribayashi had allocated only 1,860 men to its defense; but to its natural advantages had been added several hundred blockhouses, pillboxes and covered guns around its base together with an intricate system of caves in the slopes. As always, each position had to be taken separately, using a variety of weapons: mortars, tanks, rockets, flame-throwers and dynamite. When the Marines reached the caves, they went in with knives to kill the Japanese in close combat. Some of the defenders, out of ammunition, were reduced to rolling stones down the slopes, but still they fought on. By the morning of 23 February, the Marines were approaching the summit and 40 men under Lieutenant Harold Schrier carried an American flag to signify their victory. At 1020 it was raised amid cheers while fighting was still going on in the vicinity; and at noon it was replaced by a much larger flag. The planting of the second flag was photographed by Joe Rosenthal of Associated Press and the picture became probably the most famous of the entire war.

The end of the campaign was far from in sight—the worst had yet to come. Anticipating a fierce struggle, the Americans had committed the 3rd Marine Division on the same day to the middle of the front line, with the 4th on the right

Marine Corps

Imperial War Museum

58

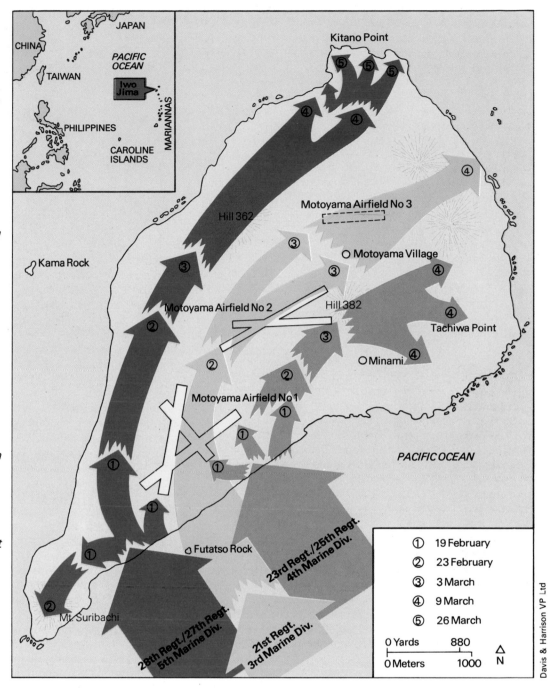

◁ *D+1 0900—the slow grind inland to capture Airfield No. 1. Iwo Jima's three air bases were the invasion's main objective. The first had been built in 1943 and over 100 Japanese aircraft were destroyed by US raids in June 1944. Before this, Japanese fighters from Iwo had intercepted B29 Super-Fortresses flying back to bases in the Marianas. Iwo was the HQ for Rear-Adm. Toshinosuke Ichimaru's 27th Naval Air Wing with 300 AA guns and 5,500 men. Over 135 pillboxes were built to defend the first airfield.*

▷ *The five bitter phases of the protracted struggle to capture Iwo's eight square miles. 1 Landings put 30,000 Marines ashore on the first day up to a half-mile inland. 2 After five days Mt Suribachi and the first airfield are secured. 3 The battle for Motoyama plateau. After ten days the 84,000 Marines regrouped in front of the second Japanese defense line. 4 It is split by Marines reaching the sea. 5 Last main Japanese pocket eliminated at Kitano.*

◁ *Marines crouch by a rock as an explosive charge destroys a cave linked to a three-tier block-house. Japanese defenses included 365 pill-boxes, 46 blockhouses, 90-odd artillery emplacements.*

and the 5th on the left, and General Schmidt had come ashore to take direct control of what was the largest group of Marines yet to fight under a single command. Only 2,630 yards of island were left but it was obvious that every one was to be paid for dearly.

Kuribayashi had systematically turned the plateau region into an armed camp. Rockets, artillery and mortars, one a 320mm weapon that lobbed 700lb shells, were in good supply and blockhouses and pillboxes were numerous. Caves were elaborate and well-fortified—one could hold 2,000 troops and had 12 exits—and the defenders were well-trained and in high morale. They were prepared to hold a position to the death, infiltrate Marine lines, or throw themselves under an enemy tank with a bomb strapped to their backs. It was all deadly, frighteningly inhuman. Admiral Turner called it 'as well defended as any fixed position that exists in the world today'.

Fortunately this kind of operation was exactly what the Marines were trained for. During the Pacific War, from one atoll to the next, the Marines endured a much more savage, personal and individual form of combat than that seen in the actions in Western Europe or North Africa, and against a fanatical enemy who would not surrender. There was no room for maneuver, or indirect approach, on this battlefield—it was one of total assault.

To reduce the casualties of the attacking forces, all the weapons of modern military technology were brought to their aid. The Japanese positions were bombarded by warships, ranging from destroyers' 5in guns to battleships' 16in guns, they were battered by heavy bombers, strafed by the rockets and machine-guns of fighters, assaulted by dive-bombers. Tanks, artillery, mortar and rocket firers hammered the positions, flame-throwers scorched them, dynamite blasted them. But the Marines knew, as they pressed ahead over the next ridge, along the next gulley, that the capture of virtually every position also involved brutal

RONSON M1 PORTABLE FLAME THROWER

Malcolm McGregor

that it was this middle zone where it was hardest to deploy tanks and artillery, or to direct the naval support fire with accuracy. Although the elements on the flanks helped, the Marines had the main job, the slow and deadly job, of clearing the area. By the tenth day of the fighting, though, the supporting fire for the 3rd Division had been substantially increased and the forward battalions found a weak spot in the Japanese line, and poured through. By evening Motoyama, now a heap of stones and rubble, was taken and the Marines could look down upon the third airfield. Once again, though, further momentum was broken by Kuribayashi's second major defense line, and there remained many areas to wipe up. Hill 382 was fiercely held by its defenders for two more days, and Hill 362 in the west was equally difficult. The whole operation was taking much longer than the 10 days Schmidt had estimated for it, and the Marines were tired and depleted in their ranks: some units were down to 30 per cent of their original strength.

On Sunday 5 March, the three divisions regrouped and rested as best they could in the face of Japanese shellings and occasional infiltration. On that day, too, the Marines had the satisfaction of seeing a B29 with a faulty fuel valve returning to Tinian from a raid on Tokyo make an emergency landing on airstrip No. 1. Iwo Jima was already fulfilling its function.

For the Japanese, the situation was serious. Most of Kuribayashi's tanks and guns and over two-thirds of his officers had been lost. His troops were in a serious position, reduced to such desperate measures as strapping explosives to their backs and throwing themselves under American tanks. The Marines were moving relentlessly forward, however slowly, and this forced a gradual breakdown in Kuribayashi's communications system. This meant that, left to their own devices, individual Japanese officers tended to revert to the offensive. This may have been more appealing to the Samurai but it exposed the greatly depleted Japanese forces to the weight of American firepower. One attack, by 1,000 naval troops on the night of 8-9 March, was easily repulsed by 4th Marine Division with Japanese losses of over 800 men. The pressure on the defending forces was starting to tell; they were losing their cohesion.

On the afternoon of 9 March, a patrol from the 3rd Marine Division reached the north-eastern coast of Iwo Jima and sent back a sample of salt water to prove that the enemy's line had been cut in two. There was no stopping the American advance but even now there was no sign of Japanese surrender—the only indication of their desperate condition was the increasing number of 'banzai' charges. Kuribayashi's

close-in fighting—with machine-gun, pistol, grenade, knife, digging-tool, even hands—before the defenders were fully overcome. This was how the hell on earth of Iwo Jima had to be taken.

The battle for the second airfield, sited almost in the dead center of the island, was typical of this form of fighting. There the Japanese had constructed hundreds of pillboxes, rabbit-holes and concealed emplacements, which defied the concentrated American fire-power for two days. On 24 February, the two battalions of the 21st Marine Regiment rushed forward to take the enemy lines with bayonet and grenade, the terrain being too difficult for tanks. Not only did the Japanese fire upon them from all their entrenched positions, but many rushed into the open and engaged in a struggle reminiscent of some medieval carnage, with the bayonet as the key weapon. Casualties rose steeply on both sides. The Marines, thrown back by this fierce counter-attack, re-formed and charged again, By nightfall of the next day, they had captured the airfield and were pressing towards Motoyama village, with only the prospect of another bitter struggle ahead: to the right of them lay the formidable Hill 382, a position which became so difficult to secure that the Marines referred to it ominously as 'the Meat Grinder'.

The fighting in the days following was the same. The Americans had to take the higher, central part of the enemy's lines first, for whenever the 4th and 5th Divisions pushed ahead on their respective flanks they were heavily punished by the Japanese who overlooked them. The problem was

△△ *A frightful but necessary weapon to smoke out Japanese bolt-holes—the Ronson M1 portable flamethrower which could squirt unlit fuel into a bunker and follow with a flame to burn up the air and asphyxiate the defenders, who were not burnt to death. Each Marine battalion had 27 of these weapons.*

△ *A Marine observer spots a Japanese position and with a grid map relays its position to US land and naval gunnery.*

▷ *Two of Iwo Jima's 22,000 Japanese defenders. Only 1,083 surrendered. The Marines suffered 26,000 dead and wounded.*

Marine Corps

RHL

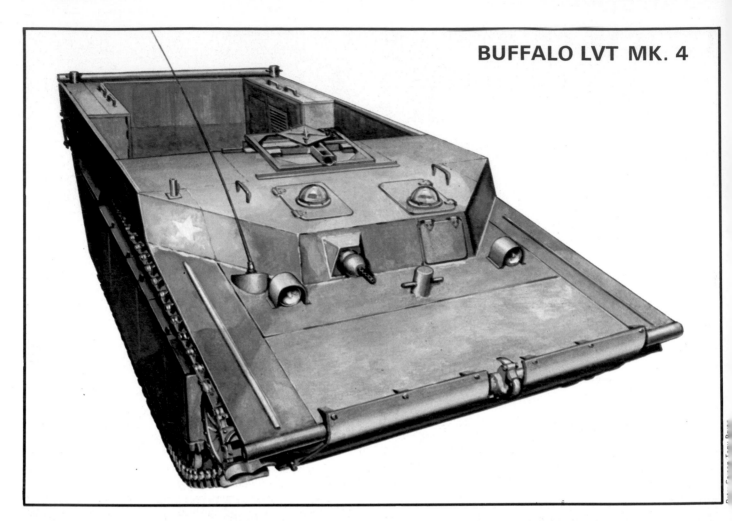

reports, however, describe the deteriorating situation: 10 March. American bombardment 'so fierce I cannot express nor write of it here'; 11 March. 'Surviving strength of northern districts (army and navy) is 1,500 men'; 14 March. Attack on northern district this morning. Much more severe than before. Around noon one part of the enemy with about 10 tanks broke through our left front line and approached to 220 yards of divisional HQ; 15 March. 'Situation very serious. Present strength of northern district about 900 men.'

On 14 March the Americans, believing all organized resistance to be at an end, declared Iwo Jima occupied and raised the Stars and Stripes. Yet underground, in their warren of caves and tunnels, the Japanese lived on. Kuribayashi told the survivors on 17 March: 'Battle situation come to last moment. I want surviving officers and men to go out and attack enemy until the last. You have devoted yourself to the Emperor. Do not think of yourselves. I am always at the head of you all.'

Clearing out pockets of organized resistance with tanks, demolition teams, rifle fire and flamethrowers took until 26 March. On this day the Japanese staged their last desperate fling when 350 troops rushed an Air Force and Seabee (Civil Engineers of the US Navy) construction camp. They were destroyed by a Marine pioneer battalion after a day of wild fighting. Kuribayashi committed suicide in the northern corner of Iwo Jima in the last few days of the battle. He promised that to help revive the Japanese army after his death, 'I will turn into a spirit'. One US Marine hoped that 'the Japs don't have any more like him'.

Only 216 Japanese had surrendered by 26 March; 20,000 were dead. In the following two months 1,600 Japanese were killed and another 370 captured as sporadic resistance was crushed. The American casualties, considering their air and sea control and their superior firepower, were equally daunting. A total of 275 officers and 5,610 men of the Marine Corps were killed and 826 officers and 16,446 men were wounded. Thirty per cent of the entire landing force and a staggering 75 per cent of the infantry regiments of the 4th and 5th Divisions were battle casualties. So depleted were some units during the action that one battalion commander commented that 'the appearance of a war dog and its handlers seemed like heavy reinforcements'. Twenty-four Medals of Honor were awarded and there were 2,648 'combat fatigue casualties'—both facts telling evidence of the gruelling nature of the battle for Iwo Jima.

Iwo Jima soon justified the strategic value which the Joint Chiefs of Staff and, in particular, the Air Force had attached to it. Before the end of the war against Japan, more than 20,000 crewmen in crippled planes had landed upon the island's airstrips; and from 7 April onwards, thanks to the efforts of the Seabee construction units, Mustang fighters were able to escort the daylight raids of the Superfortresses against Tokyo and other Japanese cities.

General Smith called the battle 'the toughest we've run across in 168 years' but also insisted that 'When the capture of an enemy position is necessary to winning a war it is not within our province to evaluate the cost in money, time, equipment, or most of all, in human life. We are told what our objective is to be and we prepare to do the job . . . .' Admiral Nimitz summed up the achievement of the assault troops: 'Among the Americans who served on Iwo Island, uncommon valor was a common virtue'. **Paul M. Kennedy**

U.S. Marine Corps Photo

US Marine photographers risked all when they went in with the assault troops. At Tarawa, a tense moment as a squad leader points to the next Japanese bunker for all-out attack. Over 3,000 Marines were killed or wounded before Tarawa fell.

U.S. Marine Corps Photo

The battle for Iwo Jima was one of the toughest assignments for US Marines in 170 years. It fell after five weeks of non-stop action. Here Pvt. Richard Klatt and Pvt. 1st Class Wilfred Voegeli burn out a Japanese bunker.

Action at sea ! One can almost hear the crash of the 40mm guns, feel the blast, sense the urgency as this gun-crew operate. (Inset) Before the invasion of Iwo Jima, the USS Salt Lake City, a Pensacola-*class* 9,100-ton heavy cruiser, bombards the island with her 8in main armament.